THE AUSTRALIAN
Women's Weekly
kids can cook

contents

The oven temperatures in this book are for conventional ovens; if you have a fan-forced oven, decrease the temperature by 10-20 degrees. A measurement conversion chart appears on the back flap of this book.

kitchen confidence

There is no down-side to teaching kids to cook. Encouraging kids to learn to cook well, not only gives them the basis for a really important life skill, but also gives them knowledge about the food they eat. Kids are more likely to eat and try different foods if they've prepared it themselves. And it's confidence-boosting, to both kids and adults alike, to make something that everybody likes and wants to eat.

KITCHEN HYGIENE

Make sure kids wash their hands thoroughly before starting to prepare the ingredients. It's also very important to wash their hands each and every time they touch raw meat, so any bacteria is not passed to another item of food. Wash hands, and under the fingernails, with soap and warm water, and dry them on a clean towel or absorbent paper. If kids have any cuts or scratches, these should be covered with either bandaids or disposable gloves. Anyone who is sick should not prepare food, and should stay out of the kitchen when food is being prepared.

Kids need to understand the importance of shopping, storing food properly, being organised, and serving and storing cooked food at the right temperature. Workspaces should be cleaned and tidied as they go to.

USING KNIVES & SAFETY

A lot depends on the child's age, maturity and kitchen experience, however, don't be afraid of letting them use sharp knives. There is more likelihood of a cut if knives are blunt, as more pressure is needed to cut through food, and this can cause the food or knife to slip. Before letting your child use a knife, assess their hand-eye coordination, concentration and the size and weight of the knife to be used, and supervise them as required. Teach your child to make a 'bridge' or a 'claw' with their hand, so they keep their fingers out of the chopping area of the knife. Using a V-slicer or mandoline, fitted with the safety guard each time, is often safer and easier for a child to use. Bench and sink height can be a problem, and sometimes a small child may need a little help; a low stool will solve the problem; make sure it's non-slip.

HANDLING HOT THINGS

When it comes to handling hot things, make sure the pan is not too heavy for the child to lift off the heat – overbalancing a pot full of hot food or water will cause major burns – and have good thick appropriately-sized oven mitts and tea towels available. Grabbing a damp tea towel to use in place of an oven mitt is a common mistake made by kids (and adults). Wet or damp patches on tea towels can turn to steam when placed on heat, causing severe scalds. It's a good idea to encourage kids when they cook to wear clothing that covers their legs, arms and chest; shoes that will protect their feet from burns from splashed hot oil or food or boiling water, or cuts from a dropped knife. Get them to tie their hair back so it won't fall into the food, or get accidently singed. Show them how their favourite TV chef dresses to protect themself in the kitchen.

GETTING READY TO COOK

Good strong basic equipment is all that's needed in a kitchen – a good cook doesn't need a huge kitchen or fancy utensils to achieve success. It's also very important to read the recipe all the way through before starting to cook anything. This means kids know what equipment they need (and aren't grabbing things at the last minute), and that the saucepans and cake pans are the right size. Reading the recipe also helps them understand the different techniques that are required and the length of time their chosen recipe will take (does it need to marinate or freeze overnight; does it need to cool between steps?).

It's smart for the beginner cook to follow the recipe, but then they can branch out and change the recipes to suit themselves and to make them their own.

SEASONING FOOD

Encourage your budding cook to taste and season food lightly as they make the recipe. When we refer to seasoning in our recipes, we mean salt and pepper. We use either fine table salt or sea salt flakes and freshly ground black pepper. Salt draws out the flavours in food, but use it sparingly as it can easily take over the natural flavours. Use pepper sparingly too, as it is 'hot' and too much can spoil a meal. If you're cooking for people you don't know, check if they have any dietary requirements – some people don't eat added salt (there are natural salts in most food) for medical reasons. Seasoning food correctly is one of those things that comes with experience – good cooks and chefs season food lightly but often during the cooking, tasting it when they can. Obviously, some food can't be tasted during the cooking because it's raw, so just add a little seasoning at these times. Just before serving the food, taste it again and season again if it's necessary. Use a clean spoon or fork each time you taste food – the success of your cooking will depend on your taste buds. Never return a used spoon or fork to the food. While lightly seasoning during cooking brings out the flavour of food, seasoning a meal is a highly personal thing: everyone has different tastebuds, and what is not enough salt for one person may be oversalted to another. Let people know you have seasoned the food, and to taste it before adding any more seasoning.

big salads

smoked salmon salad

2 large oranges (600g)

500g (1 pound) thinly sliced smoked salmon

½ small red onion (50g)

250g (8 ounces) cream cheese

2 tablespoons finely chopped fresh dill

3 cups (350g) firmly packed trimmed watercress sprigs

85g (3 ounces) bagel crisps

orange vinaigrette

2 tablespoons orange juice

2 tablespoons olive oil

1 Cut oranges in half. Put each half, cut-side down, on a chopping board. Use a small sharp knife to cut off the skin and white pith. Cut the orange flesh into 3cm (1¼-inch) pieces.

2 Chop the salmon into bite-sized pieces.

3 Peel and thinly slice onion.

4 Make orange vinaigrette.

5 Put the cream cheese and dill in a medium bowl; season with salt and pepper. Use a fork to mash together well. Lightly wet your hands and roll one teaspoonful of the cheese mixture at a time into balls.

6 Put the orange pieces, salmon, onion, cheese balls and watercress in a medium bowl; add the dressing and toss gently to combine.

7 Place the salmon salad on a large serving platter. Crumble the bagel crisps over the top.

ORANGE VINAIGRETTE Put the juice and oil in a screw-top jar; tighten the lid, then shake well. Season to taste with salt and pepper.

prep time 40 minutes **serves** 4
nutritional count per serving
36.6g total fat
(15.8g saturated fat);
2548kJ (609 cal);
26.9g carbohydrate;
40.2g protein; 6.5g fibre

note You need to pick the sprigs from one bunch of watercress for this recipe.

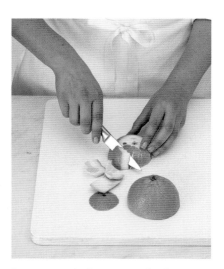

Put orange halves, cut-side down, on a chopping board. Use a small sharp knife to cut away skin and white pith.

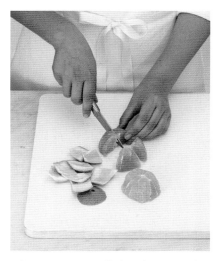

After removing all the skin, use the sharp knife to cut the orange flesh into 3cm pieces.

Lightly wet your hands and roll one teaspoonful of the dill and cream cheese mixture into balls.

Mix the spices and oil in a medium bowl; use your hands to rub the spice mixture all over the chicken.

Cook the chicken over a medium heat in a large ovenproof frying pan until browned on both sides.

Remove the seed, then use a large spoon to scoop the avocado flesh out of the skin in one piece.

chicken taco salad

2 teaspoons ground cumin

½ teaspoon cumin seeds

1 teaspoon smoked paprika

1 tablespoon olive oil

2 x 200g (6½-ounce) chicken breast fillets

3 small taco shells (33g)

1 tablespoon olive oil, extra

1 large avocado (320g)

1 small red capsicum (bell pepper) (150g)

2 medium roma (egg) tomatoes (150g)

1 lime (90g)

80g (2½ ounces) mesclun leaves

½ cup (120g) light sour cream

1½ tablespoons sweet chilli sauce

1 Preheat oven to 200°C/400°F.
2 Mix the ground cumin, cumin seeds, paprika and oil in a medium bowl; add the chicken. Use your hands to rub the cumin mixture all over the chicken; season with salt and pepper. Cover the bowl with plastic wrap; refrigerate while preparing tacos.

3 Put the tacos on an oven tray and bake according to the instructions on the packet. Cool the tacos on the tray before you touch them, then break into 3cm (1¼-inch) pieces.
4 Heat a large ovenproof frying pan on the stove over medium-high heat. Pour the extra oil into the pan, then add the chicken. Cook the chicken about 5 minutes on each side or until browned. Put the pan in the oven and roast for about 10 minutes or until the chicken is cooked through.
5 Using oven mitts, take the pan out of the oven and use tongs to transfer the chicken to a chopping board. When cool enough to handle, cut the chicken into 1cm (½-inch) slices. Cover the chicken with foil to keep it warm.
6 Cut the avocado in half from top to bottom. Place the half with the seed on a board; use a teaspoon to scoop out the seed. Use a large spoon to scoop the avocado flesh out of the skin in one piece; slice flesh thinly.

7 Cut the capsicum into quarters; cut out the seeds and membranes. Slice capsicum and tomatoes thinly.
8 Juice the lime. Put avocado, capsicum, tomato, lime juice and the mesclun in a large bowl; mix well. Add the chicken slices and taco pieces; mix gently.
9 To make the dressing, mix the sour cream and the sauce in a small bowl. Serve the salad immediately, accompanied with the dressing.

prep + cook time 50 minutes
serves 4
nutritional count per serving
30.7g total fat
(8.5g saturated fat); 1597kJ
(382 cal); 9.8g carbohydrate;
15.2g protein; 3.1g fibre

tip If you don't have a frying pan that can go in the oven, take the chicken out of the pan and put it on an oven tray before roasting in the oven.

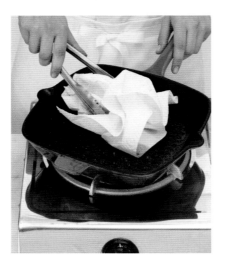
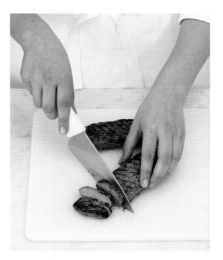

Cook the lamb in the heated grill pan until browned both sides and cooked the way you like it.

Before cooking the cheese, wipe the pan clean by using tongs to wipe the pan with absorbent paper.

Cover the lamb with foil and stand for 5 minutes before using a large sharp knife to slice the lamb thinly.

big greek lamb salad

1 clove garlic

2 teaspoons dried oregano

⅓ cup (80ml) olive oil

600g (1¼ pounds) lamb backstraps

250g (8 ounces) piece sourdough bread

¼ cup (60ml) olive oil, extra

250g (8 ounces) haloumi cheese

250g (8 ounces) cherry tomatoes

1 medium red capsicum (bell pepper) (200g)

½ small red onion (50g)

2 medium lemons (280g)

¼ cup loosely packed fresh oregano leaves

¼ cup loosely packed fresh basil leaves

1 cup watercress sprigs

1 Preheat oven to 200°C/400°F.
2 Peel then crush the garlic into a medium bowl. Add the dried oregano and the oil; season with salt and pepper. Add the lamb to the bowl, and turn to coat all over with the garlic mixture. Cover the bowl with plastic wrap; refrigerate while preparing the bread, cheese and vegetables.

3 To make the croûtons, slice the bread thinly and put it in a single layer on an oven tray. Drizzle the extra oil all over the bread. Put the tray in the oven and bake for about 15 minutes or until the bread is golden and crisp. Remove the tray from the oven, leave the croûtons to cool.
4 Meanwhile, thickly slice the cheese and halve the tomatoes. Cut the capsicum into quarters; cut away the seeds and membranes. Chop the capsicum coarsely. Peel, then coarsely chop the onion. Cut one lemon into wedges; juice the other lemon.
5 Put a large grill pan on the stove over high heat. Add the capsicum and cook for 5 minutes or until just soft. Remove capsicum from the pan using tongs and put it in a large bowl. Add the lamb to the pan and cook for about 7 minutes each side or until cooked the way you like it. Remove lamb from the pan using tongs and put it on a chopping board; cover the lamb with foil to keep it warm.

6 Remove the grill pan from the heat. Hold a piece of absorbent paper with tongs and wipe the pan clean. Put the pan back on the heat. Add the cheese to the pan and cook until golden on both sides.
7 Put the tomato, onion, cheese, lemon juice, herbs and watercress into the bowl with the capsicum; mix gently to combine.
8 Using a sharp knife, slice the lamb thinly. Top lamb with salad; serve immediately, accompanied with croûtons and lemon wedges.

prep + cook time 1¼ hours
serves 4
nutritional count per serving
51.9g total fat
(14.3g saturated fat); 3612kJ
(863 cal); 33g carbohydrate;
63.5g protein; 5g fibre

tips Place lamb in a preheated pan and don't move it until it is well sealed (at least 3 minutes) as the water released when you move the lamb will make it stick to the pan.
Haloumi cheese is best eaten straight away after cooking or it becomes rubbery and squeaky, so serve this salad immediately.

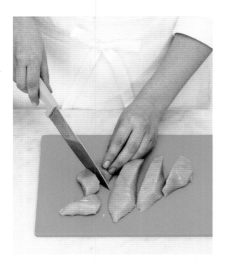

Using a sharp knife, cut the chicken into 2cm pieces.

Put half the chicken into the egg mixture. Using one hand, lift the chicken to drain off excess egg.

Place chicken in the breadcrumbs. Using your clean hand, toss chicken to coat all over in the crumbs.

chicken popcorn salad

1 medium kumara
(orange sweet potato) (400g)

2 tablespoons olive oil

200g (6½-ounce) chicken breast fillet

2 eggs

2 tablespoons milk

1 tablespoon plain (all-purpose) flour

1 cup (50g) japanese (panko) breadcrumbs

cooking-oil spray

1 packet plain microwave popcorn (100g)

1 baby cos (romaine) lettuce (240g)

250g (8 ounces) cherry tomatoes

2 teaspoons honey

2 teaspoons wholegrain mustard

¼ cup (75g) mayonnaise

¼ cup loosely packed fresh parsley sprigs

½ bunch coarsely chopped fresh chives

1 Preheat oven to 220°C/425°F.
2 Peel kumara with a vegetable peeler, then chop into chunks. Put the kumara into a medium bowl with half the oil; season with salt and pepper and mix well. Put the kumara in a single layer on an oven tray. Put the tray in the oven and roast for about 20 minutes or until kumara is soft when tested with a fork or skewer.
3 Meanwhile, cut the chicken into 2cm (¾-inch) pieces.
4 Crack the eggs, one at a time, into a small bowl or cup, then pour into a medium bowl; add the milk and whisk with a fork until combined.
5 Mix the flour and breadcrumbs in another medium bowl.
6 Brush the base of two shallow oven trays with the rest of the oil.
7 Place half the chicken into the egg mixture; use the fingers of one hand to coat the chicken in the egg, drain off excess egg. Put the chicken in the bowl with the breadcrumb mixture then, using your other hand, toss the chicken in the breadcrumbs until coated.
8 Spread the chicken in a single layer on one of the oven trays. Repeat with the remaining chicken.
9 Spray chicken with cooking-oil spray. Put the trays in the oven and roast for 10 minutes. Use tongs to turn the chicken over then roast for a further 10 minutes.
10 Meanwhile, cook the popcorn according to the instructions on the packet.
11 Separate, wash and dry the lettuce leaves. Cut some of the larger tomatoes into wedges, leave smaller ones whole.
12 To make the dressing, put the honey, mustard and mayonnaise into a small bowl and mix well.
13 Arrange the lettuce leaves on a large serving platter. Put the chicken, 2 cups of the popcorn, tomato and kumara in a medium bowl; season to taste with salt and pepper and mix well. Spoon chicken mixture over the lettuce; sprinkle over herbs. Serve salad with the dressing.

prep + cook time 1¼ hours
serves 4
nutritional count per serving
19.8g total fat
(4.5g saturated fat); 1768kJ
(423 cal); 35.8g carbohydrate;
21.8g protein; 7.3g fibre

tip Using a salad spinner is the quickest and easiest way to wash and dry lettuce leaves.

sausage and bean salad

cooling-oil spray

6 thick beef sausages (900g)

1 cup (120g) frozen peas

400g (12½ ounces) canned white beans

250g (8 ounces) cherry tomatoes

½ cup loosely packed fresh basil leaves

1 medium lemon (140g)

2 tablespoons olive oil

200g (6½ ounces) fetta cheese

1 Spray medium frying pan with cooking oil; heat on the stove over medium heat. Cook the sausages, turning occasionally with tongs, until they are browned all over and cooked through. Take the sausages out of the pan and put them on a chopping board; when cool enough to handle, slice the sausages thinly.

2 Boil or microwave the peas until tender. Pour the peas and the canned beans into a strainer over the sink; rinse under cold water then drain.

3 Cut the larger tomatoes in half; leave smaller ones whole. Tear larger basil leaves into smaller pieces.

4 To make the dressing, juice the lemon; put juice in a screw-top jar with the oil; tighten the lid then shake well. Season to taste with salt and pepper.

5 Put the sausages, peas, beans, tomato, basil and dressing in a large serving bowl. Crumble the cheese into the bowl; mix gently using two large spoons.

prep + cook time 45 minutes
serves 4
nutritional count per serving
49.7g total fat
(22.7g saturated fat); 2470kJ
(591 cal); 8.1g carbohydrate;
25.7g protein; 7.1g fibre

tip If you like, you can double the dressing recipe; it will keep in the fridge for about a week.

Cool the sausages, then use a sharp knife to slice them thinly.

Coarsely tear larger pieces of basil. Cut larger cherry tomatoes in half, leave smaller tomatoes whole.

Put the juice and oil in a screw-top jar; tighten the lid, then shake well.

crunchy chicken salad

¼ cup (60ml) light soy sauce

¼ cup (60ml) rice wine vinegar

2 tablespoons caster (superfine) sugar

¼ cup (60ml) olive oil

2 teaspoons sesame oil

¼ small cabbage (300g)

2 large carrots (300g)

1 barbecued chicken (900g)

½ cup (75g) roasted unsalted cashew nuts

100g (3 ounce) crispy fried noodles

¾ cup loosely packed fresh coriander (cilantro) leaves

1 To make the dressing, put the sauce, vinegar, sugar, olive and sesame oils in a small saucepan. Heat the pan on the stove over low heat. Cook, stirring with a wooden spoon, until the sugar has dissolved. Remove from the heat; leave the dressing to cool.
2 Meanwhile, shred the cabbage finely. Peel the carrots, then cut them into matchsticks.
3 Remove the chicken meat from the bones. Shred the chicken meat into pieces.
4 Put the cabbage, carrot, nuts, chicken, noodles, coriander and dressing in a large bowl; mix well and serve straight away.

prep + cook time 45 minutes
serves 4
nutritional count per serving
44.6g total fat
(9.8g saturated fat); 2606kJ
(623 cal); 22.2g carbohydrate;
31g protein; 6g fibre

tip Crispy fried noodles are available in the Asian aisle of supermarkets.

Using a large sharp knife, shred the cabbage as thinly as you can.

To cut the carrot into matchsticks, cut the carrot in half crossways, then cut into thin slices lengthways.

Stack the slices neatly; cut them lengthways into matchstick-sized strips. This is called 'julienne'.

Hold lettuce, cored end up, under cold running water. The water will get between the leaves, making them slip off easily and intact.

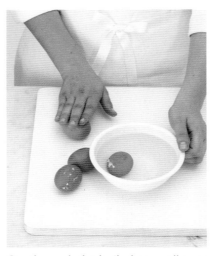

Gently crack the boiled eggs all over and put into cold water to cool.

Remove the chicken meat from the bones. Shred the chicken meat into long strips.

chicken and egg lettuce cups

1 large iceberg lettuce

4 eggs

2 medium potatoes (400g)

100g (3 ounces) thinly sliced prosciutto

1 large barbecued chicken (900g)

½ cup loosely packed fresh basil leaves

½ cup (150g) mayonnaise

2 tablespoons light sour cream

1 tablespoon honey

1 tablespoon wholegrain mustard

1 Cut the core from the lettuce. Rinse lettuce under cold running water, with the cored end facing upwards; the whole leaves should slip off easily. Put 12 medium-sized lettuce leaves with a good 'cup' shape in a bowl of iced water and keep in the fridge until required. (Keep the rest of the lettuce in a resealable plastic bag in the fridge for another use.)

2 Put the eggs and unpeeled potatoes in a medium saucepan; add enough cold water to the pan to completely cover the eggs and potatoes. Heat the pan on the stove over high heat until the water boils. Boil for 7 minutes then remove the eggs with tongs and put them in a small bowl of cold water. When cool enough to handle, gently crack the egg shells all over, leave in the water to cool.

3 Continue boiling the potatoes until they are soft when tested with a fork or skewer. Drain the potatoes in a colander over the sink, then cool.

4 Meanwhile, tear the prosciutto into pieces. Put a medium frying pan on the stove over high heat. Add the prosciutto and cook, stirring with a wooden spoon, until the prosciutto is browned and crisp. Remove the prosciutto from the pan and drain on absorbent paper.

5 Remove the chicken meat from the bones. Shred the chicken meat into pieces.

6 Peel away the egg shells. Peel potatoes. Chop the eggs, potato and basil coarsely.

7 To make the dressing, mix the mayonnaise, sour cream, honey and mustard in a large bowl; season to taste with salt and pepper. Add the chicken, egg, potato, basil and prosciutto; mix gently.

8 To serve, spoon about ½ cup of the chicken mixture into each lettuce cup.

prep + cook time 1 hour
serves 4
nutritional count per serving
38g total fat
(10g saturated fat); 2495kJ
(597 cal); 24.6g carbohydrate;
38.8g protein; 2.1g fibre

tip Trim the edges of the lettuce leaves with kitchen scissors to make them look neater.

Use one hand to dip the fish pieces into the egg mixture. Lift fish to drain off excess egg.

Use clean hand to coat the fish in the breadcrumb mixture; toss to coat the fish all over in the crumbs.

Use a V-slicer, with a safety guard, to slice the fennel as thinly as possible.

fisherman's basket salad

4 medium potatoes (800g)

2 tablespoons olive oil

2 teaspoons fresh thyme leaves

500g (1 pound) skinless, boneless firm white fish fillets

1 medium lemon (140g)

1½ cups (75g) japanese (panko) breadcrumbs

1 tablespoon plain (all-purpose) flour

2 eggs

2 tablespoons milk

2 baby fennel bulbs (260g)

1 lebanese cucumber (130g)

1 baby cos (romaine) lettuce (180g)

tartare dressing

3 pickled dill cucumbers (80g)

⅓ cup loosely packed fresh dill sprigs

1 tablespoon rinsed, drained capers

¾ cup (225g) mayonnaise

1 tablespoon lemon juice

1 Preheat oven to 200°C/400°F.
2 Peel potatoes with a vegetable peeler, then slice thickly. Cut each slice into 1.5cm (¾-inch) chips. Put the chips in a medium bowl with half the oil and 1 teaspoon of the thyme; season with salt and pepper and mix gently. Line an oven tray with baking paper. Spread the chips on the tray in a single layer. Put the tray in the oven and roast for 15 minutes.
3 Meanwhile, brush the base of a shallow oven tray with the rest of the oil. Cut the fish into 5cm (2 inch) strips.
4 Finely grate the rind from the lemon. Mix rind, breadcrumbs, flour and the rest of the thyme in a medium bowl; season with salt and pepper.
5 Crack the eggs, one at a time, into a small bowl or cup, then pour into a medium bowl; add the milk and whisk with a fork until combined.
6 Dip the fish in the egg mixture; drain off excess egg, then dip the fish into the breadcrumb mixture and toss until covered all over with crumbs. Put the fish on the oiled oven tray.
7 When the chips have been cooking for 15 minutes, put the fish in the oven with the chips. Roast for 10 minutes; use an egg slide to turn the fish and chips over. Roast a further 10 minutes or until the fish and chips are browned and cooked.

8 Meanwhile, trim the base and green parts from the fennel; use a sharp knife or V-slicer to slice the fennel as thinly as possible. Slice the cucumber into ribbons using a vegetable peeler. Separate the lettuce leaves, wash and dry leaves.
9 Make tartare dressing.
10 Layer lettuce, fennel and cucumber on serving plates; accompany with the fish and chips; serve with the dressing.

TARTARE DRESSING Put all the ingredients in a blender; blend until almost smooth. Season to taste with salt and pepper.

prep + cook time 1¼ hours
serves 4
nutritional count per serving
33.3g total fat (5.4g saturated fat); 2792kJ (667 cal); 51.4g carbohydrate; 38g protein; 7.7g fibre

tips When making the dressing, use the 'pulse' button on the blender to just combine the ingredients and lightly chop the dill cucumbers and capers. Using a salad spinner is the quickest and easiest way to wash and dry the lettuce leaves.

Tear the bread into small pieces about the same size as the nuts.

Pan-fry the bread and nut mixture until golden, then immediately turn out onto an oven tray to cool.

Cook lamb in a large frying pan until browned underneath. Turn to cook on the other side.

char-grilled vegetable salad with lamb cutlets

1 day-old bread roll (50g)

30g (1 ounce) each of pine nuts, macadamias and walnuts

⅔ cup (160ml) olive oil

2 cloves garlic

2 teaspoons finely grated lemon rind

2 medium zucchini (240g)

2 baby eggplants (120g)

2 medium red capsicums (bell peppers) (400g)

olive-oil spray

12 french-trimmed lamb cutlets (600g)

⅓ cup (25g) finely grated parmesan cheese

½ cup finely chopped fresh basil

2 tablespoons finely chopped fresh flat-leaf parsley

1 Tear the bread roll into small pieces (about the same size as the nuts). Put the bread and nuts on an oven tray; drizzle with 1 tablespoon of the oil and rub well with your hands to coat all over in the oil.

2 Heat a large frying pan over medium-high heat; panfry the bread and nut mixture, stirring constantly, for about 5 minutes or until golden. Remove from pan immediately; spread out on oven tray to cool.

3 Meanwhile, peel and crush the garlic. Whisk half the garlic with the lemon rind and 1 tablespoon of the oil in a large bowl until combined; season.

4 Slice the zucchini and eggplants thickly. Cut the capsicums into quarters; remove the seeds and membranes. Chop the capsicum coarsely. Add the vegetables to the garlic mixture and mix well. Char-grill vegetables in a grill pan until browned and tender.

5 After the vegetables have been cooking for 5 minutes, spray the same large frying pan with the olive-oil spray. Heat the pan over medium-high heat. Season the cutlets with salt and pepper and add to the pan; cook for about 5 minutes or until cooked as you like them. Put the lamb on a plate and cover loosely with foil; set aside to rest for 2 minutes.

6 Meanwhile, to make the chunky pesto, put the cooled bread and nut mixture, the rest of the oil and garlic, the cheese and herbs in a large bowl; mix well. Season to taste with salt and pepper.

7 Serve the lamb and vegetables with the pesto.

prep + cook time 35 minutes
serves 4
nutritional count per serving
60.7g total fat
(10g saturated fat); 2900kJ
(693 cal); 12.9g carbohydrate;
23.2g protein; 5g fibre

tips We used a mixture of walnuts, macadamias and pine nuts for this recipe but you can use any combination of nuts you like.

Run a vegetable peeler down the length of the cucumber to make long, thin ribbons.

Soaking skewers prevents them from burning during cooking. Soak them in cold water for at least 30 minutes.

Thread one piece of onion onto a skewer, fold one piece of salmon, back and forth, onto the skewer.

cucumber salad with teriyaki salmon skewers

2.5cm (1-inch) piece fresh ginger (15g)

½ cup (125ml) teriyaki sauce

½ teaspoon sesame oil

700g (1½ pounds) skinless salmon fillet

2 green onions (scallions)

cucumber salad

1 tablespoon mirin

1 teaspoon japanese soy sauce

1 tablespoon rice vinegar

½ teaspoon sesame oil

2 lebanese cucumbers (260g)

1 tablespoon toasted sesame seeds

1 Soak 12 bamboo skewers in water for 30 minutes.
2 Meanwhile, peel then grate the ginger. Combine the ginger, teriyaki sauce and oil in a large bowl. Cut the salmon into strips about 8mm (½-inch) thick. Add the salmon to the bowl and mix well to coat the salmon in the teriyaki mixture. Cover the bowl with plastic wrap; refrigerate until ready to use.

3 Meanwhile, trim and cut the onions into 4cm (1½-inch) pieces.
4 Make the cucumber salad.
5 Thread a piece of onion onto a skewer, then thread a piece of salmon onto the skewer, folding it back and forth at 2cm (¾-inch) intervals. Repeat with another piece of salmon then onion. Repeat this process to make 12 skewers.
6 Heat a large frying pan over medium-high heat; cook the salmon skewers for about 5 minutes or until the salmon changes colour. Serve salmon skewers with cucumber salad; sprinkle over sesame seeds.

CUCUMBER SALAD Whisk the mirin, soy sauce, rice vinegar and sesame oil in a medium bowl until combined. Use a vegetable peeler to slice the cucumber into long thin ribbons. Add the cucumber to the bowl with sauces; mix well.

prep + cook time 45 minutes (+ standing & refrigeration)
serves 4
nutritional count per serving
15.2g total fat (3.1g saturated fat); 1281kJ (306 cal); 2.9g carbohydrate; 37g protein; 1.3g fibre

tips Soaking the bamboo skewers in cold water before using them stops them from burning when you cook the skewers. You can use metal skewers instead, if you have them; be careful when turning as they will be very hot. You can also grill (broil) the salmon skewers, if you prefer.
To toast sesame seeds, place seeds in a small frying pan, toast over medium heat, shaking pan occasionally, until golden and fragrant, about 3-5 minutes.

serving idea Serve with steamed jasmine rice.

soups & casseroles

chicken, corn and noodle soup

1 medium brown onion (150g)

2 cloves garlic

3cm (1¼-inch) piece fresh ginger (15g)

420g (13½ ounces) canned corn kernels

1 tablespoon vegetable oil

1 litre (4 cups) chicken stock

2 cups (500ml) water

125g (4 ounces) canned creamed corn

4 green onions (scallions)

125g (4 ounces) dried wheat noodles

350g (11 ounces) chicken breast fillets

2 tablespoons japanese soy sauce

100g (3 ounces) baby spinach leaves

1 Peel then finely chop the brown onion. Peel then crush the garlic. Peel then finely grate the ginger. Drain the liquid from the canned corn in a strainer over the sink; rinse with water, drain.

2 Heat oil in a large saucepan on the stove over medium heat for 1 minute. Add the brown onion, garlic and ginger to the pan. Stir with a wooden spoon for about 5 minutes or until the onion is soft.

3 Add the stock, the water and both corns to the pan. Put the lid on the pan. Turn the stove to high and heat until the mixture boils.

4 Meanwhile, trim and coarsely chop the green onion. Keep the green parts in a small bowl; add the white parts to the pan. Reduce the heat to medium-low. Simmer, uncovered, for 5 minutes.

5 Carefully break the noodles in half and add to the pan. Simmer, uncovered, for about 2 minutes. Stir to separate the noodles.

6 Slice chicken thinly; add to the pan with the soy sauce. Simmer, uncovered, about 1 minute or until the chicken is cooked. (Add extra soy sauce to taste, if needed.)

7 Stir in the spinach. Using a ladle, divide the soup into four serving bowls. Sprinkle with the rest of the green onion.

prep + cook time 30 minutes
serves 4
nutritional count per serving
7.8g total fat
(1.5g saturated fat); 1664kJ
(398 cal); 47.9g carbohydrate;
30.7g protein; 6.3g fibre

Break the noodles in half and add to the simmering soup mixture.

Using a large bladed knife, slice the chicken breast thinly.

Once the chicken is just cooked (changed from pink to white) stir in the spinach.

Use your fingers to shred the meat from a barbecued chicken.

Use a large spoon to remove the cooked bacon and onion mixture from the pan to a medium bowl.

Add flour to the melted butter in the saucepan. Stir until it becomes a smooth paste, then add the milk.

bacon, potato and chicken chowder

3 medium potatoes (600g)

6 green onions (scallions)

2 cloves garlic

4 rindless bacon slices (260g)

40g (1½ ounces) butter

⅓ cup (50g) plain (all-purpose) flour

3 cups (750ml) milk

3 cups (750ml) salt-reduced chicken stock

2 cups (320g) shredded barbecued chicken

1 Peel the potatoes; cut into 1.5cm (¾-inch) cubes. Put the potato into a medium bowl and add enough cold water to the bowl so the potato is covered.
2 Trim and coarsely chop the green onion; keep the white and green parts separate in two small bowls. Peel then crush the garlic.
3 Chop the bacon coarsely. Place in a large saucepan on the stove over medium heat. Stir the bacon with a wooden spoon for about 5 minutes or until browned.
4 Add the white parts of the green onion and the garlic to the bacon. Stir about 3 minutes or until the onion is soft. Remove the saucepan from the heat. Use a large spoon to remove the bacon mixture from the pan and put it into a medium bowl.
5 Melt the butter in the same saucepan on the stove over medium heat. Add the flour; stir with a wooden spoon until the mixture becomes a smooth paste. Pour the milk in slowly, a little bit at a time, and stir until the mixture is smooth before adding more milk. Stir in the stock; stir the mixture until it boils and thickens.
6 Drain the potato; add potato to the pan. Put the lid on and simmer, covered, for about 10 minutes or until the potato is soft when tested with a fork or skewer. Stir the soup a few times to make sure it is not sticking to the base of the pan.
7 Stir the chicken and bacon into the potato mixture; simmer, uncovered, for about 2 minutes or until the chicken is hot. Season the soup with salt and pepper to taste.
8 Using a ladle, divide the soup into four serving bowls. Sprinkle the soup with the rest of the chopped green onion.

prep + cook time 40 minutes
serves 4
nutritional count per serving
27.8g total fat
(14.3g saturated fat); 2468kJ
(590 cal); 32.7g carbohydrate;
45.2g protein; 2.7g fibre

notes Buy a barbecued chicken or use leftover chicken from a roast for this recipe. Leftover chicken is delicious on sandwiches with mayonnaise, avocado and lettuce for a school lunch.
Add a drained large can of corn kernels or 1 cup frozen corn kernels to the soup with the chicken if you like.
If you have leftover soup, you may need to add a little water or extra chicken stock to the soup when you reheat it, as it will thicken overnight in the refrigerator. Always reheat leftover soup until it boils.

Cut the pumpkin in half crossways. Scoop out the seeds using a spoon, then peel all the pumpkin.

Test the vegetables with a fork or skewer. They should be easy to pierce when they are cooked.

Blend the soup in the saucepan with a stick blender until the mixture is smooth.

sweet potato, pumpkin and potato soup

1kg (2 pounds) butternut pumpkin

500g (1 pound) kumara (orange sweet potato)

500g (1 pound) potatoes

1 medium brown onion (150g)

1 clove garlic

30g (1 ounce) butter

1.25 litres (5 cups) salt-reduced chicken stock

1 cup (250ml) reduced-fat pouring cream

1 tablespoon finely chopped fresh chives

1 Cut the pumpkin in half crossways with a large sharp knife. Scoop out the seeds with a spoon, then peel the pumpkin with a vegetable peeler or sharp knife. Chop the pumpkin coarsely.
2 Peel the kumara and potatoes with a vegetable peeler. Rinse well under cold water. Chop coarsely.
3 Peel then coarsely chop the onion. Peel then crush the garlic.
4 Melt the butter in a large saucepan on the stove over medium heat. Add onion and garlic to the pan; stir with a wooden spoon about 5 minutes or until the onion is soft.
5 Stir the stock into the pan. Put the lid on the saucepan. Turn the stove on to high and heat until the mixture boils. Carefully add the pumpkin, kumara and potato to the pan. Put the lid back on and heat until the mixture boils. Reduce the heat to medium-low. Simmer for about 15 minutes or until the vegetables are soft when tested with a fork or skewer. Remove the soup from the heat; stand for 10 minutes with the lid off to cool slightly.

6 Blend the soup in the pan with a stick blender until smooth. (Or, ladle about one-third of the vegetables and liquid into a blender or food processor. Blend or process until the soup is smooth. Pour the soup into a large jug or bowl. Repeat with the remaining soup mixture, then return the soup to the pan.)
7 Add half the cream to the soup. Season to taste with salt and pepper. Turn the stove on to medium heat; stir the soup until heated through.
8 Using a ladle, divide the soup into six serving bowls. Spoon one tablespoon of the remaining cream on top of each bowl; sprinkle with the chives.

prep + cook time 50 minutes
serves 6
nutritional count per serving
16.2g total fat
(10.7g saturated fat); 1342kJ
(321 cal); 32.7g carbohydrate;
9.6g protein; 4.3g fibre

tip Use kitchen scissors to snip the chives.

mild chilli con carne with guacamole

800g (1½ pounds) boneless beef shin or chuck steak

1 tablespoon vegetable oil

1 medium brown onion (150g)

2 cloves garlic

30g (1 ounce) taco seasoning

400g (12½ ounces) canned diced tomatoes

1 tablespoon tomato paste

2 cups (500ml) salt-reduced beef stock

250g (12½ ounces) canned kidney beans

310g (10 ounces) canned corn kernels

1 small green capsicum (bell pepper) (150g)

8 small flour tortillas (200g)

guacamole

1 large roma (egg) tomato (90g)

¼ medium red onion (40g)

1 medium avocado (250g)

1 tablespoon lime juice

2 tablespoons coarsely chopped fresh coriander (cilantro)

1 Cut the beef into 4cm (1½-inch) pieces. Heat the oil in a large saucepan on the stove over medium-high heat for 1 minute. Add half the beef; cook, stirring, until the beef is browned all over. Remove beef from the pan with tongs, and place in a bowl. Repeat with the rest of the beef.
2 Cut the onion in half lengthways. Peel away the skin and trim the root end, then cut lengthways into 12 wedges. Peel and crush the garlic. Add the onion and garlic to the pan; stir for about 5 minutes or until the onion is soft.
3 Return the beef and any juices to the pan. Stir in taco seasoning, undrained canned tomatoes, paste and stock. Turn the stove to high and heat until the mixture boils. Reduce the heat to as low as possible on the smallest element. Put the lid on the pan; simmer for about 1¾ hours or until the beef is tender when tested with a fork.
4 Make the guacamole.
5 Rinse and drain the beans and corn in a strainer over the sink. Cut the capsicum into quarters;

cut out the seeds and membranes. Chop the capsicum coarsely. Add the beans, corn and capsicum to the pan. Simmer, covered, a further 10 minutes or until the capsicum is tender. Season to taste.
6 Warm tortillas following packet directions. Serve chilli con carne with guacamole and tortillas.

GUACAMOLE Finely chop the tomato. Peel and finely chop the onion. Cut the avocado in half. Remove the seed with a small spoon. Scoop the flesh out of the skin with a large spoon; place into a medium bowl. Mash the flesh a little with a fork, leaving it chunky. Stir in the tomato, onion, juice and coriander; season to taste with salt and pepper. Cover; refrigerate until serving time.

prep + cook time 2½ hours
serves 4
nutritional count per serving
33.5g total fat
(8.5g saturated fat); 3076kJ
(736 cal); 45.9g carbohydrate;
57.9g protein; 9.2g fibre

Use a fork to test if the beef is tender. The fork should easily 'cut' through the meat, breaking it apart.

Remove the avocado seed, then use a large spoon to scoop the flesh out of the skin.

Roughly mash the avocado in a bowl with a fork. The mixture should be chunky.

Using a large sharp knife, cut the gai lan stems from the leaves.

Remove the wilted gai lan leaves from the pan with a slotted spoon.

Rinse and drain the noodles in a colander or sieve in the sink.

braised honey and soy pork fillet steaks

2 cloves garlic

5cm (2-inch) piece fresh ginger (25g)

1 tablespoon peanut oil

4 pork scotch fillet steaks (750g)

⅓ cup (80ml) light soy sauce

¼ cup (90g) honey

½ cup (125ml) water

800g (1½ pounds) gai lan

450g (14½ ounces) fresh hokkien noodles

1 Preheat oven to 160°C/325°F.
2 Peel then crush the garlic. Peel then grate the ginger.
3 Heat the oil in a small flameproof baking dish on the stove over medium-high heat for 1 minute. Carefully place the pork in the dish in a single layer. Cook about 2 minutes or until browned underneath. Turn the pork with tongs. Cook for a further 2 minutes or until browned. Remove from the stove; add the garlic and ginger to the dish. Stir in the sauce, honey and the water.

4 Cover the dish with a tight-fitting lid or two layers of foil. Place the dish in the oven. Cook the pork for 1½ hours.
5 Carefully remove the lid or foil away from you to allow the steam to escape. Place the uncovered dish back in the oven and cook, for a further 30 minutes or until the pork is tender when tested with a fork (the pork should break apart easily). Remove the dish from the oven. Cover to keep warm.
6 Meanwhile, half-fill a medium saucepan with water. Cover with the lid. Heat on the stove over high heat until the water boils.
7 Cut the gai lan stems from the leaves. Trim the stems and add to the saucepan of boiling water; boil, uncovered, for 1 minute. Remove stems from the saucepan with a slotted spoon; transfer to a plate. Cover with foil to keep warm. Add the leaves to the water; boil, uncovered, about 30 seconds or until just wilted. Remove the leaves from the pan with a slotted spoon; place on the plate. Cover to keep warm.

8 Add the noodles to the same saucepan of boiling water; cook about 2 minutes, stirring noodles with a fork to separate. Drain the noodles into a colander in the sink. Return the noodles to the same pan; add ½ cup of the pan juices from the pork. Toss the noodles to coat with the juices.
9 Serve the noodles and gai lan topped with the pork. Drizzle over the rest of the pan juices.

prep + cook time 2¼ hours
serves 4
nutritional count per serving
12.3g total fat
(3.3g saturated fat); 2721kJ
(651 cal); 79.7g carbohydrate;
52.2g protein; 5.2g fibre

notes Use vegetable oil instead of peanut oil if you prefer. Pork scotch fillet steaks are also known as pork neck steaks. Gai lan is also known as chinese broccoli; use choy sum if you can't get it.

Using a large sharp knife, cut the beef into 5cm pieces.

Brown the beef all over in the pan; the beef is just browning at this stage, not cooking through.

Peel and halve the onion lengthways through the root. Cut the onion lengthways into 12 wedges.

beef massaman curry with jasmine rice

800g (1½ pound) piece gravy beef or chuck steak

1 tablespoon peanut oil

2 medium brown onions (300g)

½ cup (150g) massaman curry paste

2 cups (500ml) coconut cream

2 cinnamon sticks

3 star anise

¼ cup (55g) firmly packed light brown sugar

1 tablespoon lime juice

2 tablespoons fish sauce

1⅓ cups (330ml) water

2 medium potatoes (400g)

2 tablespoons roasted salted peanuts

steamed jasmine rice

1½ cups (300g) jasmine rice

1½ cups (375ml) water

1 Cut the beef into 5cm (2-inch) pieces. Heat the oil in a large saucepan on the stove over medium-high heat for 1 minute. Using tongs, carefully place the beef in the pan. Cook the beef for about 5 minutes or until browned all over, turning beef with tongs. Remove the beef from the pan with tongs or a slotted spoon; place in a medium bowl.
2 Cut onions in half lengthways. Peel away the skin, then trim the root end. Cut onions lengthways into 12 wedges. Add the onion and curry paste to the pan; stir with a wooden spoon for about 5 minutes or until the onion is soft. Stir in the coconut cream, spices, sugar, juice, sauce and the water. Turn the stove to high; heat until the mixture boils.
3 Return the beef and any juices in the bowl to the pan. Reduce the heat to as low as possible on the smallest burner or element. Put the lid on the pan; simmer for 1½ hours.
4 Peel the potatoes with a vegetable peeler. Cut each potato into six pieces and add to the pan; simmer, covered, a further 20 minutes or until potato and beef are tender when tested with a fork.
5 Make steamed jasmine rice.
6 Season the curry to taste with salt and pepper. Discard the cinnamon sticks and star anise.
7 Sprinkle the curry with the nuts; accompany with the rice.

STEAMED JASMINE RICE Put rice in a strainer, rinse under cold running water until the water runs clear; drain. Put rice in a medium saucepan; add the water. Put a tight-fitting lid on the pan and turn the stove on to high. When the water boils, reduce the heat to as low as possible. Simmer, covered, for about 8 minutes or until the rice is tender. The best way to test if it's cooked is to remove a few grains with a spoon, cool them slightly, then taste them. If it's done, put the lid back on and remove the pan from the stove. Keep the pan covered to keep the rice warm. Just before serving, fluff the rice with a fork.

prep + cook time 2½ hours
serves 4
nutritional count per serving
58.5g total fat
(29.2g saturated fat); 4832kJ
(1156 cal); 95.8g carbohydrate;
58.5g protein; 8.3g fibre

tip The saucepan lid must be tight to stop the steam escaping while cooking the rice. If the lid is wobbly, put a layer or two of foil under the lid to make it sit tightly on the pan.

To make the dumplings, use your fingertips to rub the butter into the flour, so the mixture is crumbly.

Using a table knife, cut through the dumpling mixture to form a soft, sticky dough.

Discard the dark green top from the leek; cut leek in half lengthways and wash under cold running water.

lamb casserole with herb dumplings

1kg (2 pounds) boneless lamb shoulder

1 tablespoon olive oil

1 medium leek (350g)

1 medium carrot (120g)

2 celery stalks (300g)

40g (1½ ounce) packet french onion soup mix

2 cups (500ml) salt-reduced chicken stock

½ cup (125ml) water

20g (¾ ounce) butter

herb dumplings

1 cup (150g) self-raising flour

40g (1½ ounces) cold butter

1 egg

2 tablespoons finely chopped fresh flat-leaf parsley

2 tablespoons finely chopped fresh chives

⅓ cup (80ml) milk

1 Preheat oven to 160°C/325°F.
2 Cut excess fat from the lamb and discard it. Cut the lamb into 4cm (1½-inch) pieces.
3 Put 2 teaspoons of the oil in a small flameproof baking dish. Heat the oil on the stove over medium-high heat for 1 minute. Carefully place half the lamb in the dish; cook for about 5 minutes or until browned all over, turning lamb with tongs. Remove the lamb from the dish with tongs; place in a medium bowl. Repeat with the rest of the oil and lamb.
4 Meanwhile, cut the dark green top from the leek and cut off the root end. Cut the leek in half lengthways. Peel off the outer layer and throw it away. Wash the leek under cold running water to remove any dirt between the leaves, especially at the top. Drain well. Cut the leek into slices.
5 Peel then thickly slice the carrot. Trim and coarsely chop the celery.
6 Add leek, carrot and celery to the dish with the lamb; stir with a wooden spoon until combined. Stir in the soup mix then the stock and the water. Cover dish with a lid or tightly with two layers of foil. Place the dish in the oven; cook for 1¾ hours.
7 When the lamb has cooked for 1½ hours, make the dumplings.
8 Remove the dish from the oven. Stir the lamb mixture well. Season to taste. Drop rounded dessertspoons of the dumpling mixture on top of the lamb mixture about 2cm (¾ inch) apart.
9 Melt the butter in a small saucepan on the stove over low heat. Use a pastry brush to brush the tops of the dumplings with the butter. Return the dish to the oven. Cook, uncovered, for about 20 minutes or until the dumplings are browned and cooked through.

DUMPLINGS Place the flour in a medium bowl. Chop the butter finely. Use your fingertips to rub the butter into the flour. Lightly beat the egg, and add with the herbs and milk in the centre of the flour. Use a butter knife to cut through the mixture and make a soft, sticky dough.

prep + cook time 2¾ hours
serves 6
nutritional count per serving
22.9g total fat
(11.2g saturated fat); 1960kJ
(469 cal); 24.2g carbohydrate;
39.9g protein; 3.6g fibre

tip You can buy chopped lamb for stewing from the butcher or supermarket to save time.
serving idea Serve with steamed green beans or broccoli.

bakes

carbonara pasta bake with peas

375g (12 ounces) small pasta shells

1 cup (120g) frozen peas

6 shortcut rindless bacon slices (150g)

cooking-oil spray

1¼ cups (310ml) pouring cream (see tips)

1 egg

1 cup (80g) coarsely grated parmesan cheese

1 Preheat oven to 200°C/400°F.
2 Half-fill a large saucepan with water; cover with a lid. Heat on the stove over high heat until the water boils. Add the pasta; cook, uncovered, until tender (check the packet instructions for how long this should take). About 1 minute before the pasta is ready, add the peas to the pan; cook for 1 minute. Place a colander over a large heatproof bowl in the sink.

Pour the pasta and peas into the colander; reserve about ¼ cup of the cooking liquid in the bowl and drain the rest down the sink. Return pasta and peas to the pan.
3 Meanwhile, trim any fat from the bacon; chop bacon coarsely. Spray a small frying pan with the cooking oil. Heat the pan on the stove for 30 seconds over medium-high heat. Add the bacon; cook, stirring with a wooden spoon, for about 4 minutes or until the bacon is browned.
4 Whisk the cream, egg and half the cheese in a medium bowl or jug with a fork until combined.
5 Pour the cream mixture over the pasta and peas. Add bacon and 2 tablespoons of the pasta cooking liquid; mix well. Spoon pasta mixture into a 2-litre (8-cup) ovenproof dish or into four 2-cup (500ml) ovenproof dishes; sprinkle with the rest of the cheese.

6 Place the dish on an oven tray; place in the oven and bake for about 25 minutes or until the cheese has melted and the top is golden brown.

prep + cook time 45 minutes
serves 4
nutritional count per serving
46g total fat (28.1g saturated fat); 3415kJ (817 cal); 68.2g carbohydrate; 30.7g protein; 5.3g fibre

tips It is fine to use just the one 300ml carton of cream. Cook the pasta 'al dente'; this means there should be a slight resistance in the centre when the pasta is chewed. It should not be soft.

Drain the pasta in a colander over a large heatproof bowl in the sink, to catch the cooking liquid.

Stir the egg mixture, bacon and 2 tablespoons of the pasta cooking liquid into the pasta in the pan.

Spoon the pasta mixture into an ovenproof dish; sprinkle cheese over the top of the pasta.

chicken and ricotta lasagne

1 barbecued chicken (900g)

500g (1 pound) firm ricotta cheese

2 cups (200g) pizza cheese

cooking-oil spray

2 cups (520g) bottled tomato pasta sauce with basil

4 fresh lasagne sheets

24 large basil leaves

1 Preheat oven to 200°C/400°F.
2 Using hands, remove the chicken meat from the bones; discard the bones. Shred the chicken meat into pieces.
3 Put the ricotta and half of the pizza cheese in a medium bowl; season with salt and pepper, mix well with a fork.
4 Spray a 2-litre (8-cup) ovenproof dish with cooking-oil spray. Pour ½ cup of the pasta sauce into the dish; spread it over the base. Put one lasagne sheet on top of the sauce (if it's larger than the dish, cut the sheet to fit). Sprinkle about one-third of the chicken over the lasagne sheet; dollop spoonfuls of the ricotta mixture (about ⅔ cup) over the chicken and spread out using the back of the spoon. Top with 6 basil leaves; pour ½ cup of the pasta sauce over the top. Repeat the layers with the rest of the lasagne sheets, chicken, ricotta mixture, basil and

pasta sauce to make two more layers, finishing with the fourth lasagne sheet on top.
5 Spread the rest of the ricotta mixture over the top lasagne sheet; top with the last 6 basil leaves. Sprinkle with the rest of the pizza cheese.
6 Place the dish on an oven tray; place into the oven and bake for about 35 minutes or until the pasta is cooked and the cheese is golden brown.

prep + cook time 55 minutes
serves 6
nutritional count per serving
29.8g total fat
(14.2g saturated fat); 1906kJ
(456 cal); 16.6g carbohydrate;
37.6g protein; 2.5g fibre

tip Tomato pasta sauce is also known as passata.

Spread sauce over base of the dish; cover sauce with lasagne sheet, cut sheet to fit the dish, if needed.

Dollop spoonfuls of the ricotta mixture over the chicken then spread with the back of the spoon.

Arrange basil leaves over the top of the cheese mixture, pour more of the pasta sauce over the top.

chicken and pumpkin pasta bake

700g (1½-pound) piece pumpkin

cooking-oil spray

½ barbecued chicken (450g)

375g (12 ounces) large rigatoni pasta

150g (4½ ounces) baby spinach leaves

⅔ cup (160ml) pouring cream

½ cup (50g) pizza cheese

2 tablespoons pine nuts

1 Preheat oven to 200°C/400°F.
2 Place the piece of pumpkin in a medium microwave-safe bowl, cover the bowl with plastic wrap. Microwave on HIGH (100%) for 3 minutes. When cool enough to handle; remove the pumpkin from the bowl with tongs and put it on a board. Cut away the skin; scoop out the seeds and throw them away. Cut the pumpkin into slices.

3 Spray an oven tray with the cooking oil; place the pumpkin slices on the tray, in a single layer. Spray with the cooking oil and season with salt and pepper. Bake for about 20 minutes or until tender when tested with a fork.
4 Meanwhile, using your hands, remove the chicken meat from the bones; break the chicken meat into large chunks.
5 Half-fill a large saucepan with water; put a lid on the pan. Heat on the stove over high heat until the water boils. Add the pasta; cook, uncovered, until it is tender (check the instructions on the packet for how long this should take). Place a colander over a large heatproof bowl in the sink. Pour the pasta into the colander; reserve about ¼ cup of the cooking liquid in the bowl and drain the rest down the sink. Return pasta to the pan.

6 Add the chicken, spinach, cream and the reserved cooking liquid to the pasta in the pan; mix well. Season to taste with salt and pepper.
7 Spoon the pasta mixture into a 2-litre (8-cup) ovenproof dish. Tuck the pumpkin into the pasta mixture; sprinkle with the cheese and nuts.
8 Place the dish on an oven tray; place into the oven and bake for about 15 minutes or until the cheese has melted and the top is golden.

prep + cook time 45 minutes
serves 4
nutritional count per serving
36.5g total fat (17g saturated fat); 3231kJ (773 cal); 74.6g carbohydrate; 33.6g protein; 6.2g fibre

tip When removing plastic wrap from a hot microwave bowl, remove the wrap away from you to allow the steam to escape.

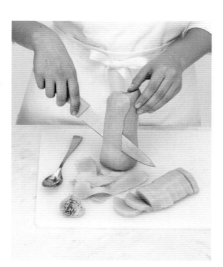

Cut the skin from the pumpkin. Scoop out the seeds, then cut the pumpkin into slices.

Drain the pasta in a colander over a large heatproof bowl in the sink, to catch the cooking liquid.

Spoon the pasta mixture into the dish then tuck the pumpkin amongst the pasta.

lemony tuna and pasta bake

400g (12½ ounces) broccoli

375g (12 ounces) large spiral pasta

425g (1½ ounces) canned tuna in olive oil

1¼ cups (310ml) pouring cream (see tips)

2 teaspoons finely grated lemon rind

2 tablespoons lemon juice

⅔ cup (70g) pizza cheese

1 medium lemon (140g)

1 Preheat oven to 200°C/400°F.
2 Using your hands, break the broccoli into small florets.
3 Half-fill a large saucepan with water; put a lid on the pan. Heat on the stove over high heat until the water boils. Add the pasta; cook, uncovered, until it is tender (check the instructions on the packet for how long this should take). About 3 minutes before the pasta is ready, add the broccoli; cook for another 3 minutes. Place a colander over a large heatproof bowl in the sink. Pour the pasta and broccoli into the colander; reserve about ¼ cup of the cooking liquid in the bowl and drain the rest down the sink. Return pasta and broccoli to the pan.
4 Meanwhile, drain the tuna; add to the pasta with the cream, lemon rind, lemon juice and 2 tablespoons of the cooking liquid from the pasta. Season with salt and pepper; mix well. Spoon the pasta mixture into four 2-cup (500ml) ovenproof dishes; sprinkle with the cheese.
5 Place the dishes on an oven tray; place into the oven and bake for about 30 minutes or until the cheese has melted and the top is golden brown.
6 Cut the lemon into wedges; serve alongside the pasta bake.

prep + cook time 45 minutes
serves 4
nutritional count per serving
50.5g total fat
(26.7g saturated fat); 3795kJ
(908 cal); 67.1g carbohydrate;
42.8g protein; 7.3g fibre

tips It is fine to use just the one 300ml carton of cream. You need 2 lemons, one for the rind and juice and the other one for the wedges.

Cut off most of the core, then using your hands, break the broccoli into small florets.

Drain the pasta and broccoli in a colander over a large heatproof bowl in the sink, to catch the cooking liquid.

Finely grate the rind from a lemon using a microplane or fine grater.

Using a sharp knife, trim excess fat from the chicken thigh fillets.

Place rice in base of bowl; top with half the chicken mixture and half the peas. Repeat the layering.

Place a folded tea towel over the plate and bowl, hold them together firmly; flip biryani over onto plate.

butter chicken biryani

1½ cups (300g) basmati rice

2¼ cups (560ml) water

600g (1¼ pounds) chicken thigh fillets

1 tablespoon vegetable oil

350g (11 ounces) bottled butter chicken simmer sauce

½ cup (125ml) water, extra

cooking-oil spray

1½ cups (180g) frozen peas

¼ cup (20g) flaked almonds

½ cup loosely packed fresh coriander (cilantro) leaves

1 Put the rice in a strainer, rinse rice under cold running water until the water runs clear; drain. Put rice in a medium saucepan; add the water. Put a tight-fitting lid on the pan; heat on the stove over high heat until the water boils. When boiling, reduce the heat to as low as possible. Simmer, covered, for about 14 minutes or until the water is absorbed and the rice is tender. The best way to test if it's cooked is to remove a few grains with a spoon, cool them slightly, then taste them.

If it's done, remove the pan from the stove. Fluff the rice with a fork.
2 Spoon the rice onto an oven tray and spread it out to cool slightly (and stop it over-cooking).
3 Meanwhile, trim the fat from the chicken; cut the chicken into bite-sized pieces.
4 Heat half the oil in a large frying pan on the stove over high heat for 1 minute. Carefully add half the chicken; cook, stirring occasionally with a wooden spoon, for about 3 minutes or until browned. Remove the chicken with a slotted spoon and put in a medium bowl. Repeat with remaining chicken and oil.
5 Return all the chicken to the pan with the simmer sauce and the extra water. Reduce the heat to low and simmer, uncovered, for 5 minutes.
6 Meanwhile, preheat the oven to 180°C/350°F.
7 Spray a 2-litre (8-cup) ovenproof bowl, or pudding basin, with cooking oil; cut strips of baking paper to line bowl or basin. Put 1 cup of the rice in the base of the bowl; top with half the chicken mixture, then half the peas. Top

with 1 cup of the rice, then the rest of the chicken mixture and the rest of the peas. Top with the rest of the rice. Cover the bowl with greased foil.
8 Place the bowl on an oven tray; place into the oven and bake for about 30 minutes or until heated through.
9 Meanwhile, toast the nuts in a medium frying pan on the stove over low heat, stirring, about 3 minutes or until golden. Remove the nuts from the pan and put them in a small bowl.
10 Take the tray out of the oven. Stand the biryani in the bowl for 5 minutes, then carefully turn out onto a serving plate. Sprinkle the biryani with the coriander and nuts before serving.

prep + cook time 1 hour
serves 4
nutritional count per serving
24.8g total fat
(6.9g saturated fat); 2738kJ
(655 cal); 67.4g carbohydrate;
37.7g protein; 6.1g fibre

serving idea Serve with lemon wedges and pappadums.

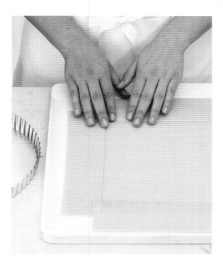
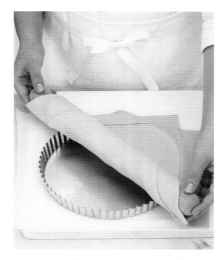

Put the pastry strips, overlapping slightly, around the edges of the pastry sheet. Press firmly to seal.

Using a rolling pin, carefully lift the pastry into the tin.

Press pastry into base and around side of tin; press pastry slightly over edge of tin for a little extra height.

ham and spinach quiche

2 sheets shortcrust pastry

150g (4½ ounces) baby spinach leaves

120g (4 ounces) sliced leg ham

6 eggs

1¾ cups (430ml) pouring cream

1 cup (120g) coarsely grated cheddar cheese

1 Preheat oven to 200°C/400°F. Put a 24cm (9½-inch) round loose-based fluted tart tin on an oven tray.

2 Put one sheet of pastry on a board. Cut the other pastry sheet into four strips; place a strip, slightly overlapping, over each side of the whole pastry sheet and press down firmly to seal the joins. Carefully lift the pastry into the tin; gently press the pastry into the base and around the side of the tin, pressing the excess pastry slightly above the edge of the tin (this gives a little extra height to the pastry in case the pastry shrinks during baking). Trim away excess pastry.

3 Cover the pastry with a piece of baking paper; fill it with dried beans or uncooked rice. Put the tray in the oven; bake 15 minutes. Take the tin out of the oven. Gently lift the paper and beans out of the pastry case. Put the pastry case back in the oven and bake about 10 minutes or until the pastry is golden brown. Take the tin out of the oven. (This is known as 'blind baking', see tips.) Reduce oven temperature to 160°C/325°F.

4 Meanwhile, wash and drain the spinach. Put the damp spinach in a large microwave-safe bowl, cover the bowl with plastic wrap. Microwave on HIGH (100%) for about 2 minutes or until the spinach is wilted. Drain the spinach in a colander in the sink. When the spinach is cool enough to handle, squeeze out as much of the water from the spinach as you can.

5 Coarsely chop the ham. Break the eggs, one at a time, into a small cup or bowl then pour into a large bowl. Add the cream; whisk until combined. Stir in the spinach, ham and cheese; season with pepper.

6 Pour egg mixture into pastry case. Put the quiche in the oven and bake for about 50 minutes or until the filling is set.

7 Take quiche out of the oven; stand 10 minutes before serving.

prep + cook time 1¼ hours
serves 6
nutritional count per serving
59g total fat (34.7g saturated fat);
3001kJ (718 cal);
27g carbohydrate;
21g protein; 1.7g fibre

tips Pastry is often baked blind, so keep the beans and rice that you used especially for this, as after they've been used to blind bake, they can't be used for any other cooking or eating. After you've finished with the beans and/or rice (a mixture is fine); spread them out on a flat tray to cool completely. Store them in a jar or airtight container. Label them to save confusion; they'll keep for years.
When removing plastic wrap from a hot microwave bowl, remove the wrap away from you to allow the steam to escape.

Rinse the beans under cold running water, then drain away excess water.

Add the beef mince to the pan; cook, breaking up any large lumps with the wooden spoon.

Stir the beans and the undrained tomato into the beef mixture.

mexican bake

750g (1½ pounds) canned kidney beans

1 large brown onion (200g)

2 cloves garlic

1 tablespoon olive oil

300g (9½ ounces) minced (ground) beef

1½ tablespoons ground cumin

1 tablespoon ground coriander

2 teaspoons dried oregano

400g (12½ ounces) canned diced tomatoes

¾ cup (180ml) water

80g (2½ ounces) corn chips

1 cup (120g) coarsely grated cheddar cheese

¼ cup loosely packed fresh coriander (cilantro) leaves

1 Empty the beans into a large colander; rinse under cold running water until the water runs clear. Drain well. Peel then finely chop onion. Peel then crush garlic.
2 Heat the oil in a large saucepan on the stove over medium heat for 1 minute. Add the onion; stir with a wooden spoon for about 5 minutes or until the onion is soft. Increase the heat to high and add the beef to the pan. Cook, stirring, for about 2 minutes or until mince is browned, breaking up any large lumps with the spoon.
3 Stir the garlic, cumin, ground coriander and oregano into the pan. Cook, stirring, for 1 minute or until fragrant.
4 Add the undrained canned tomatoes, the beans and the water to the pan; reduce the heat and let it simmer, covered with a lid, for about 30 minutes or until thickened slightly. Season to taste with salt and pepper.
5 Turn the grill (broiler) on to high.

6 Spoon the beef mixture into a 1.5-litre (6-cup) shallow ovenproof dish and put the dish on an oven tray. Put the corn chips on top of the beef mixture; sprinkle with the cheese. Place the dish under the grill for about 3 minutes or until the cheese melts and starts to bubble. Sprinkle the bake with the fresh coriander leaves to serve.

prep + cook time 50 minutes
serves 4
nutritional count per serving
26.8g total fat
(12.1g saturated fat); 2255kJ
(539 cal); 34.7g carbohydrate;
33.9g protein; 11.6g fibre

tips You can make the recipe ahead of time up to the end of step 2. You'll need to reheat the beef mixture either on the stove or in the microwave before completing steps 3 and 4.
serving ideas Serve with store-bought guacamole dip and sour cream.

beef and baked bean pies

2 celery stalks (300g)

1 small leek (200g)

1 tablespoon olive oil

400g (12½ ounces) minced (ground) beef

420g (13½ ounces) canned baked beans in tomato sauce

2 tablespoons barbecue sauce

¼ cup (60ml) water

2 sheets puff pastry

1 egg

1 Preheat oven to 220°C/425°F.
2 Trim then finely chop the celery. Cut the dark green top from the leek and cut off the root end. Cut the leek in half lengthways. Peel off the outer layer and throw it away. Wash the leek under cold running water to remove any dirt between the leaves, especially at the top. Drain well. Slice the leek thinly.
3 Heat the oil in a large saucepan on the stove over medium-low heat for 1 minute. Add the celery and leek; cook for about 10 minutes, stirring every now and then with a wooden spoon, until the vegetables soften. Increase the heat to high and add the beef to the pan. Cook, stirring, for about 2 minutes or until the beef is browned, breaking up any large lumps with the back of the spoon. Add the beans, sauce and the water to pan; stir until mixture is hot. Season to taste with salt and pepper.
4 Spoon the beef mixture into four 1¼-cups (310ml) ovenproof dishes. Cut one pastry sheet into four squares. Dip your finger or a pastry brush in a little water and moisten the edges of the pastry squares. Cover each dish with a square of pastry (wet-side down) and press down firmly to seal the pastry edges against the sides of the dishes.
5 Cut out shapes (or use a star or other-shaped cutter) from remaining pastry sheet. Beat egg lightly with a fork; brush some of the egg on the back of the shapes and stick to the top of the pies. Brush egg all over pie tops.
6 Place the dishes on an oven tray; place in the oven and bake for about 15 minutes or until pastry is puffed and golden. Stand the pies for at least 10 minutes before serving.

prep + cook time 45 minutes
serves 4
nutritional count per serving
31.7g total fat
(5.8g saturated fat); 2572kJ
(615 cal); 48.7g carbohydrate;
30.3g protein; 7.8g fibre

tip You can also make one large family-sized pie in a 1-litre (4-cup) ovenproof dish; cut the pastry to fit the top of the dish.

serving idea Serve with mashed peas (see recipe page 85).

Discard the dark green top from the leek; cut leek in half lengthways and wash under cold running water.

Cut the pastry sheet into four squares. Brush the edges with a little water to moisten.

Cover each dish with a pastry square; press down firmly to seal the edges.

To make breadcrumbs, remove crusts from bread slices with a serrated bread knife. Process until fine.

Add the breadcrumbs to the chopped parsley and mix well.

Remove the sausages from the pan with tongs and put on a plate to cool before cutting.

sausage and bean bake

1.2kg (2½ pounds) canned cannellini beans

2 teaspoons olive oil

4 thick lamb sausages (600g)

1 large brown onion (200g)

2 cloves garlic

400g (12½ ounces) canned cherry tomatoes

¼ cup (60ml) water

¾ cup (50g) stale breadcrumbs

⅓ cup finely chopped fresh flat-leaf parsley

1 Preheat oven to 200°C/400°F.

2 Empty the beans into a large colander; rinse under cold running water until the water runs clear. Drain well.

3 Heat the oil in a large frying pan on the stove over medium-low heat for 1 minute. Add sausages; cook, turning occasionally, for about 15 minutes or until browned all over and cooked through.

4 Meanwhile, peel then finely chop the onion. Peel then crush the garlic.

5 Remove the sausages from the pan with tongs and put on a plate. When cool enough to handle; slice sausages thickly.

6 Increase the heat to medium. Add the onion to the same pan; stir with a wooden spoon for about 5 minutes or until the onion is soft. Add the garlic; cook, stirring, for 1 minute.

7 Return the sausages to the pan; add beans, undrained canned tomatoes and the water, stir until heated through. Season to taste with salt and pepper. Spoon the sausage mixture into a shallow 1.5-litre (6-cup) ovenproof dish or four 375ml (1½-cup) dishes.

8 Combine the breadcrumbs and parsley in a small bowl; sprinkle all over the sausage mixture. Place the dish on an oven tray; place in the oven and bake for about 15 minutes or until the breadcrumbs are golden and crisp.

prep + cook time 35 minutes
serves 4
nutritional count per serving
30.6g total fat
(12.2g saturated fat); 2433kJ
(582 cal); 28.5g carbohydrate;
45.2g protein; 7.6g fibre

spinach and prosciutto gnocchi

100g (3 ounces) thinly sliced prosciutto

1kg (2 pounds) potato gnocchi

150g (4½ ounces) baby spinach leaves

1 cup (250g) mascarpone cheese

½ cup (40g) finely grated parmesan cheese

1 Using hands, tear the prosciutto into small pieces.

2 Turn the grill (broiler) on to high.

3 Half-fill a large saucepan with water; put a lid on the pan. Heat on the stove over high heat until the water boils. Add the gnocchi and cook, uncovered, until the gnocchi float to the surface and are tender (check the instructions on the packet for how long this should take). Place a colander over a large heatproof bowl in the sink. Pour the gnocchi into the colander; reserve ⅓ cup of the cooking water in the bowl and drain the rest down the sink. Return the gnocchi to the pan.

4 Add the prosciutto, spinach, mascarpone and the reserved cooking liquid to the gnocchi; season with pepper and stir well.

5 Spoon the gnocchi mixture into a shallow 1.5-litre (6-cup) ovenproof dish; sprinkle with the parmesan.

6 Place the dish under the grill for about 4 minutes or until the top is golden.

prep + cook time 15 minutes
serves 6
nutritional count per serving
28.6g total fat (17.4g saturated fat); 2165kJ (518 cal); 49.4g carbohydrate; 13.7g protein; 4.5g fibre

tip Do not add any salt to the gnocchi mixture as the prosciutto and parmesan are quite salty. Ready-made gnocchi is available from the refrigerated section of most supermarkets.

serving ideas Fry some tomato slices and fresh basil leaves until just softened to serve with this bake, if you like.

Cook the gnocchi in boiling water until they float to the surface.

Drain gnocchi through a colander over a large heatproof bowl in the sink, to catch the cooking liquid.

Return the drained gnocchi to the pan; stir in the prosciutto, spinach, mascarpone and reserved liquid.

one pot

summer spaghettini

375g (12 ounces) spaghettini pasta

½ small red onion (50g)

1 clove garlic

250g (8 ounces) cherry tomatoes

½ cup (130g) rocket pesto

¼ cup (60ml) olive oil

100g (3 ounces) cherry bocconcini cheese

⅓ cup loosely packed fresh basil leaves

1 Half-fill a large saucepan with water; put a lid on the pan. Heat on the stove over high heat until the water boils. Add the pasta; cook, uncovered, until it is tender (check the instructions on the packet for how long this should take). Place a colander over a large heatproof bowl in the sink. Pour the pasta into the colander; reserve about ¼ cup of the cooking water in the bowl and drain the rest down the sink. Return pasta to the pan.

2 Meanwhile, peel then finely chop onion and garlic together on a board; place in a medium bowl. Coarsely chop tomatoes; place in a bowl with onion mixture.

3 Put the pan with the pasta back on the stove over low heat. Reheat the pasta, stirring, until hot. Stir in the reserved cooking liquid, pesto, oil, tomato and onion mixture, and cheese. Season to taste with salt and pepper.

4 Divide the pasta into serving bowls; tear the basil leaves and sprinkle over the pasta to serve.

prep + cook time 20 minutes
serves 4
nutritional count per serving
31.5g total fat
(7.4g saturated fat); 2650kJ
(634 cal); 66.4g carbohydrate;
18.5g protein; 5.2g fibre

note Spaghettini is a very thin spaghetti. It is available from Italian grocery stores and most large supermarkets.

Drain the pasta in a colander over a large heatproof bowl in the sink, to catch the cooking liquid.

Finely chop the onion and garlic together on a chopping board.

Coarsely chop the tomatoes and combine with the onion mixture.

Cook the chorizo in the frying pan, over medium-high heat, until browned all over.

Make two layers of potato, onion, capsicum and chorizo in the pan.

Pour in the egg mixture. Cook the frittata over a low heat until starting to set on the bottom of the pan.

spanish-style frittata

You need an ovenproof frying pan with a 20cm (8 inch) base measurement for this recipe.

1 medium red onion (170g)

1 tablespoon olive oil

2 cured chorizo sausages (200g)

3 medium waxy potatoes (600g)

olive-oil spray

150g (4½ ounces) bottled roasted red capsicum (bell pepper), drained

2 teaspoons smoked paprika

¼ cup coarsely chopped fresh flat-leaf parsley

9 eggs

1 Cut the onion in half lengthways. Peel away the skin, trim root end. Cut the onion lengthways into 12 wedges.
2 Heat oil in the frying pan on the stove over medium-high heat for 1 minute. Add onion to the pan; cook, stirring with a wooden spoon, for about 3 minutes or until the onion is soft and golden.

Remove the onion with a slotted spoon and put it in a small heatproof bowl.
3 Meanwhile, cut the chorizo into thick slices. Add to the pan and cook for about 2 minutes each side or until browned. Remove with a slotted spoon and put it in another small heatproof bowl.
4 Peel the potatoes with a vegetable peeler then slice them thinly with a mandoline, V-slicer or sharp knife. Add to the same pan; pour enough cold water into the pan to completely cover the potato. Put a lid on the pan (if you don't have a lid, cover tightly with foil) and heat until the water boils. Boil for about 2 minutes or until the potato is barely tender. Pour the potato into a colander in the sink and drain well.
5 Preheat oven to 140°C/280°F.
6 Spray the same pan with the olive-oil spray. Layer the potato, onion, capsicum and chorizo in the pan; sprinkle over paprika and parsley, season with salt and pepper.

7 Crack the eggs, one at a time, into a small bowl or cup, then pour into large jug and beat lightly with a whisk to combine. Pour over chorizo and vegetable layer in pan. Cook egg mixture in the pan on the stove over low heat for about 6 minutes or until it is starting to set on the bottom of the pan.
8 Put the pan in the oven and cook the frittata for about 45 minutes or until golden and set. Using oven mitts, carefully remove the pan from the oven and stand for 10 minutes before cutting into wedges.

prep + cook time 1¼ hours (+ standing) **serves** 8
nutritional count per serving
15.9g total fat (4.9g saturated fat); 1031kJ (246 cal); 10.7g carbohydrate; 14.5g protein; 1.7g fibre

five-spice pork and vegie stir-fry

450g (14½ ounces) fresh hokkien noodles

150g (4½ ounces) snow peas

115g (3½ ounces) baby corn

1 small carrot (70g)

2 green onions (scallions)

2 tablespoons vegetable oil

300g (9½ ounces) minced (ground) pork

1½ teaspoons five-spice powder

½ cup (125ml) oyster sauce

½ teaspoon sesame oil

1 Put the noodles in a medium heatproof bowl; pour in enough boiling water to completely cover the noodles. Stir the noodles with a fork to separate them. Put a colander in the sink; pour the noodles into the colander and drain well.

2 Meanwhile, trim the snow peas then cut in half. Cut the corn in half lengthways. Peel the carrot with a vegetable peeler, then cut into matchsticks. Trim the onions then slice them thinly on an angle.

3 Heat half the vegetable oil in a wok on the stove over medium-high heat for 1 minute. Add the pork; cook, stirring with a wooden spoon, for about 4 minutes or until browned, breaking up any large lumps with the back of the spoon. Add the five-spice; cook for about 1 minute or until fragrant. Remove the pork from the wok and put it in a medium heatproof bowl.

4 Heat the rest of the vegetable oil in the wok for 1 minute, add the corn and carrot; stir-fry for 1 minute. Add the snow peas; stir-fry for about 1 minute. Return the pork to the wok with the noodles; stir to combine. Add the sauce and sesame oil; stir-fry for 1 minute or until hot.

5 Divide stir-fry into serving bowls; sprinkle with the onion.

prep + cook time 30 minutes
serves 4
nutritional count per serving
17.1g total fat
(3.5g saturated fat); 2424kJ
(580 cal); 73.7g carbohydrate;
29.2g protein; 4.8g fibre

tip The trick to stir-frying is having all the ingredients chopped, weighed and measured before you start cooking. This is known as 'mise en place', and translates to 'everything in its place' and ready to go.

Trim the snow peas, peeling the stem and string away from the peas, then cut snow peas in half.

To cut the carrot into matchsticks, cut the carrot in half crossways, then cut into thin slices lengthways.

Stack the slices neatly; cut them lengthways into matchstick-sized strips. This is called 'julienne'.

one-pot fry-up

4 thin beef sausages (120g)

4 rindless bacon slices (260g)

100g (3 ounces) portobello mushrooms

100g (3 ounces) haloumi cheese

250g (8 ounces) cherry tomatoes

200g (6½ ounces) baby spinach leaves

4 eggs

1 Heat a deep, large frying pan on the stove over medium heat. Add the sausages to the pan; cook, turning with tongs, for about 10 minutes or until browned and cooked through. Remove sausages from the pan; drain on absorbent paper.

2 Increase the heat to medium-high and add the bacon to the pan. Cook for about 6 minutes, turning, until browned both sides. Remove bacon from the pan and drain on absorbent paper.

3 Meanwhile, cut the mushrooms into quarters. Cut the cheese into small cubes. Add the mushrooms to the pan; cook, stirring, for about 4 minutes or until the mushrooms are golden and the water has evaporated. Remove mushrooms from the pan and put in a small bowl. Add the cheese to the pan and cook for about 30 seconds each side or until golden. Remove from the pan and put in a small bowl.

4 Add the tomatoes to the pan; cook, stirring, for about 2 minutes or until the skins start to split. Add the spinach to the pan and cook, stirring, for about 20 seconds or until wilted. Remove the pan from the heat.

5 Carefully put the sausages, bacon, mushrooms and cheese back into the pan with the tomatoes and spinach; push the ingredients to the side slightly to make four small holes for the

eggs. Crack the eggs, one at a time, into a small cup or bowl, then slide into the holes in the pan. Put a lid on the pan or tightly cover with foil. Turn the stove down to medium-low heat. Cook for about 5 minutes or until the egg whites are cooked but the yolks are still runny (or until the eggs are cooked as you like them). Season to taste with salt and pepper.

prep + cook time 30 minutes
serves 4
nutritional count per serving
23g total fat
(10.2g saturated fat); 1434kJ
(343 cal); 3.2g carbohydrate;
29.9g protein; 2.4g fibre

tip Use chipolata sausages if you prefer them.

Cook the tomatoes until the skins begin to shrivel and split, then add the spinach and stir until wilted.

Push the mixture slightly to the side of the frying pan to make four holes for the eggs to slide into.

Crack the eggs, one at a time, into a small bowl or cup, then slide into the holes in the pan.

Squeeze the sausage meat from the casings into a medium bowl.

Using wet hands, roll the sausage mixture into meatballs.

Cook the meatballs over a medium-high heat until browned all over.

sausage meatball pasta

1 large brown onion (200g)

1 tablespoon olive oil

600g (1¼ pounds) thick italian pork or beef sausages

2 cloves garlic

400g (12½ ounces) canned chopped tomatoes

1½ cups (375ml) beef stock

½ cup (125ml) water

350g (11 ounces) rigatoni pasta

¼ cup loosely packed fresh oregano leaves

⅓ cup (25g) finely grated parmesan cheese

1 Peel then finely chop the onion. Heat the oil in a large heavy-based saucepan on the stove over medium heat for 1 minute. Add the onion to the pan; cook, stirring with a wooden spoon, for about 4 minutes or until soft. Remove the onion from the pan and put it in a small heatproof bowl.

2 Meanwhile, squeeze sausage meat from casings into a medium bowl. Throw away casings (the skin that covers the sausages). Roll the sausage mixture into 2.5cm (1-inch) balls with wet hands.

3 Increase the heat to medium-high. Add the meatballs to the pan; cook for about 5 minutes, turning, until browned all over.

4 Meanwhile, peel then crush the garlic. Add the garlic to the pan with the onion and undrained canned tomatoes, stock and the water; heat until the mixture boils.

5 Reduce heat to medium-low; add the pasta to the pan and cover with a lid. Cook, stirring every few minutes to stop the pasta from sticking to the base of the pan, for about 15 minutes or until the pasta is tender and the liquid has been absorbed. Remove the pan from the heat; leave the lid on the pan and stand for 5 minutes before serving. Season to taste with salt and pepper; stir in oregano.

6 Divide pasta and meatballs into serving bowls; sprinkle with the cheese.

prep + cook time 45 minutes
serves 4
nutritional count per serving
43.2g total fat
(17.7g saturated fat); 3428kJ
(820 cal); 70.9g carbohydrate;
33.3g protein; 7.8g fibre

risi e bisi

A classic of the northern Italian city of Venice, this Venetian dish has the rather boring name of 'rice and peas', when translated into English.

200g (6½ ounces) thickly sliced pancetta

1 medium brown onion (150g)

1 tablespoon olive oil

1 clove garlic

1½ cups (300g) arborio rice

1 litre (4 cups) salt-reduced chicken or vegetable stock

2 cups (500ml) water

200g (6½ ounces) frozen peas

¼ cup (20g) finely grated parmesan cheese

1 teaspoon finely grated lemon rind

1 tablespoon lemon juice

½ cup coarsely chopped fresh mint

1 Use a sharp knife to cut the rind from the pancetta; cut the pancetta into small sticks (known as batons). Peel then finely chop the onion. Heat the oil in a large saucepan on the stove over medium-high heat. Add the pancetta and onion to the pan. Cook, stirring with a wooden spoon, for about 5 minutes or until the pancetta is golden and the onion is soft.

2 Meanwhile, peel then crush the garlic. Add the garlic to the pan with the rice, stock, and the water; heat until the mixture boils.

3 Reduce the heat to low; simmer the mixture for about 12 minutes or until the rice is tender, stirring every few minutes. (The best way to test if the rice is tender is to remove a few grains with a spoon, cool slightly then taste them.)

4 Stir in the peas. Cook for a further 2 minutes until hot. Stir the cheese, lemon rind, lemon juice and half the mint into the rice mixture. Season to taste with salt and pepper. Divide the rice mixture into serving bowls; sprinkle with the rest of the mint and serve straight away.

prep + cook time 40 minutes
serves 6
nutritional count per serving
9.3g total fat
(3.1g saturated fat);
1400kJ (335 cal);
45.7g carbohydrate;
5.3g protein; 3.6g fibre

Cut the rind from pancetta then cut the pancetta into small sticks.

Stir the rice, stock and the water into the onion mixture.

When the rice is tender, stir in the peas; cook until the peas are hot.

oven-roasted

crunchy buttermilk chicken

5½ cups (220g) corn flakes

1½ tablespoons finely chopped fresh thyme

⅓ cup (50g) plain (all-purpose) flour

1 teaspoon paprika

1 teaspoon garlic powder

1 teaspoon sea salt

½ teaspoon ground black pepper

¾ cup (180ml) buttermilk

8 chicken drumsticks (1.2kg)

2 corn cobs (800g), trimmed

2 rindless bacon slices (130g)

80g (2½ ounces) mixed salad leaves

1 Preheat oven to 200°C/400°F.

2 Put the corn flakes in a large resealable plastic bag; crush with a rolling pin until coarse. Place the corn flakes crumbs into a medium bowl with the thyme.

3 Mix the flour, paprika, garlic powder, salt and pepper in a shallow bowl. Pour the buttermilk into another shallow bowl.

4 Take the skin off the drumsticks (or ask the butcher, or an adult, to do this for you). Coat the drumsticks all over in the flour mixture, shake off any excess flour. Dip the drumsticks in the buttermilk, then dip in the corn flake mixture, turning until covered all over.

5 Line a large oven tray with a piece of baking paper. Put the drumsticks on the tray, in a single layer; place in the oven and roast for about 40 minutes or until cooked through. If the chicken is getting too brown during cooking, cover the tray with foil. To test if the chicken is cooked, remove one piece of chicken and place it on a plate. Cut into the thickest part of the chicken to the bone – the meat should not be pink.

6 Meanwhile, using a heavy flat-bladed knife, cut the corn cobs in half (or ask an adult to do it for you). Cut the bacon slices in half lengthways. Wrap the bacon strips around the corn cobs; secure the bacon ends with a toothpick. Season with salt and pepper.

7 Place the corn on an oven tray; place in the oven for the last 20 minutes of the chicken cooking time.

8 Serve the chicken and corn with salad leaves.

prep + cook time 1 hour
serves 4
nutritional count per serving
5.8g total fat (1.9g saturated fat);
2115kJ (506 cal);
87.4g carbohydrate;
20.7g protein; 8.7g fibre

Put the corn flakes in a large plastic resealable bag; crush with a rolling pin until coarse.

Dip the drumsticks into the flour mixture, the buttermilk, then the corn flake mixture to coat.

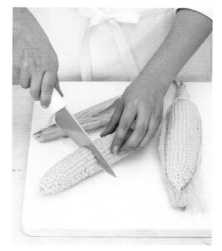

Cut the corn cobs in half with a large heavy knife, or get an adult to cut the corn for you.

sticky, smoky pork ribs with slaw

2 tablespoons light brown sugar

1 tablespoon smoked paprika

1 teaspoon sea salt

½ teaspoon ground black pepper

1.5kg (3 pounds) american-style pork rib racks

smoky barbecue sauce

6 cloves garlic

¾ cup (165g) firmly packed light brown sugar

¾ cup (225g) apple sauce

½ cup (125ml) cider vinegar

¾ cup (210g) tomato sauce (ketchup)

3 teaspoons smoked paprika

3 teaspoons onion powder

3 teaspoons worcestershire sauce

slaw

1 clove garlic

¼ cup (75g) mayonnaise

¼ cup (60ml) buttermilk

500g (1 pound) green cabbage

¼ cup coarsely chopped fresh flat-leaf parsley

1 Mix the sugar, paprika, salt and pepper in a small bowl. Rub the mixture all over the ribs; put the ribs in a single layer in a large baking dish. Stand for 30 minutes at room temperature.

2 Meanwhile, make the smoky barbecue sauce.

3 Preheat oven to 200°C/400°F.

4 Put the ribs in the oven; roast for 15 minutes. Carefully remove dish from the oven. Using a pastry brush, brush about one-quarter of the barbecue sauce all over both sides of the rib racks. Turn the ribs over; put the dish back in the oven. Roast for a further 15 minutes, then brush again with more sauce. Continue to roast the ribs for a further 30 minutes, turning and brushing with sauce after 15 minutes. If the ribs are getting too brown or beginning to burn, cover the dish with foil.

5 Meanwhile, make the slaw.

6 Using a sharp knife, cut the racks into individual ribs between the bones (or get an adult to do this for you). Serve the ribs with the slaw and the reserved barbecue sauce.

SMOKY BARBECUE SAUCE Peel then crush the garlic. Mix the garlic with the rest of the ingredients in a medium heavy-based saucepan. Heat the sauce on the stove over medium-high heat until the mixture boils. Reduce the heat to low; simmer for about 20 minutes, stirring occasionally with a wooden spoon, or until the sauce is slightly thick. Remove the pan from the heat; leave the sauce to cool. Keep aside ⅓ cup of the sauce for serving.

SLAW Peel then crush the garlic. Whisk the garlic, mayonnaise and buttermilk in a large bowl until combined. Using a sharp knife or a V-slicer, finely shred the cabbage then add to the bowl with the parsley; season to taste with salt and pepper and mix well.

prep + cook time 1¾ hours (+ standing) **serves 4**
nutritional count per serving
14.6g total fat
(4.3g saturated fat); 2299kJ
(550 cal); 76.9g carbohydrate;
26.4g protein; 6.7g fibre

Brush the ribs generously with the barbecue sauce.

Continue to roast the ribs, brushing with sauce and turning the ribs every 15 minutes.

Using a sharp knife, cut the rib racks into individual ribs, between the bones.

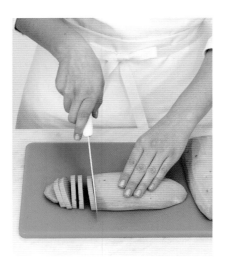

Cut kumara in half lengthways. Cut each half into 1cm-thick slices.

Cut each slice into 1cm-thick chips.

Use tongs to flip the fish over to brown on the other side.

fish and kumara chips

3 large kumara (orange sweet potato) (1.5kg)

2 tablespoons vegetable oil

2 teaspoons ground cumin

2 teaspoons ground coriander

1 teaspoon ground turmeric

1 teaspoon coarse cooking salt

2 tablespoons sesame seeds

⅓ cup (25g) japanese (panko) breadcrumbs

2 tablespoons plain (all-purpose) flour

1 egg

4 x 100g (3-ounce) skinless, boneless firm white fish fillets

lime and coriander yogurt

½ cup (140g) thick greek-style yogurt

1½ tablespoons lime juice

1 tablespoon finely chopped fresh coriander (cilantro)

1 Preheat oven to 200°C/400°F.
2 Use a vegetable peeler to peel the kumara. Cut the kumara in half lengthways, then cut each half into 1cm (½-inch) thick slices. Cut the slices into 1cm (½-inch) thick chips. Put the chips in a medium bowl with half the oil; season with salt and pepper and mix well to coat the chips in oil.
3 Line an oven tray with baking paper; put the chips, in a single layer, on the tray. Put the tray in the oven and roast for about 15 minutes or until chips are golden and cooked through.
4 Meanwhile, mix the spices, salt, sesame seeds and breadcrumbs in a wide shallow bowl. Put the flour in another shallow bowl. Beat the egg in another shallow bowl with a fork. Coat the fish all over in the flour, shake off any excess flour. Dip the fish in the egg then dip in the breadcrumb mixture, turning until the fish is covered all over.
5 Heat the rest of the oil in a large ovenproof frying pan on the stove over medium heat for 1 minute. Add the fish to the

pan and cook about 30 seconds or until browned underneath. Turn the fish with tongs or an egg slide. Cook about 30 seconds or until browned on the other side.
6 Put the frying pan with the fish in the oven; roast for about 2 minutes or until the fish is barely cooked through.
7 Meanwhile, make lime and coriander yogurt. Serve the fish and chips accompanied with the yogurt.

LIME AND CORIANDER YOGURT
Mix all the ingredients in a small bowl. Season to taste with salt and pepper.

prep + cook time 35 minutes
serves 4
nutritional count per serving
14.9g total fat
(4.3g saturated fat); 2167kJ
(518 cal); 58.5g carbohydrate;
33.3g protein; 7g fibre

tip If you don't have a frying pan that can go in the oven, take the fish out of the frying pan and put it on an oven tray before roasting in the oven.

vegetables

rosemary potato wedges

4 medium potatoes (800g)

1½ tablespoons olive oil

1 tablespoon fresh rosemary leaves

1 Preheat oven to 240°C/475°F.
2 Wash and scrub the potatoes well to remove any dirt from the skins; pat them dry with absorbent paper.
3 Cut the potatoes in half; cut each half into four wedges. Put the wedges in a medium bowl with the oil and rosemary; season with salt and pepper. Turn the wedges so they are covered all over with the oil and seasoning.
4 Put the wedges in a large shallow baking dish then put the dish in the oven. Bake about 35 minutes or until the wedges are golden and tender.

prep + cook time 45 minutes
serves 4 as a side
nutritional count per serving
7.3g total fat (1g saturated fat); 832kJ (199 cal); 26.4g carbohydrate; 4.8g protein; 3.2g fibre

tip We used sebago potatoes because they are a good all-round potato.

serving ideas Goes well with roasted chicken, grilled steaks, lamb or pork chops.

Scrub the potatoes. Pat them dry with absorbent paper.

Cut the potatoes in half. Cut each half into four wedges.

Mix wedges with the oil, rosemary, salt and pepper in a medium bowl so the wedges are coated all over.

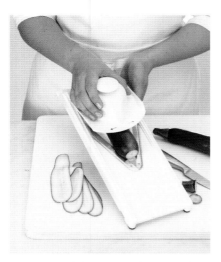
Use a mandoline or V-slicer to slice the zucchini and potato thinly.

Cut potatoes lengthways so they are of a similar height to the zucchini.

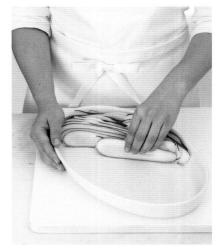
Stand the zucchini and potato in the dish so they stand lengthways on their edge.

potato, zucchini and pesto bake

¾ cup (180ml) milk

¾ cup (180ml) pouring cream

2 tablespoons basil pesto

2 large zucchini (300g)

4 medium potatoes (800g)

½ cup (40g) finely grated parmesan cheese

1 tablespoon pine nuts

1 Preheat oven to 200°C/400°F. Grease the base and insides of a shallow 1.5-litre (6-cup) ovenproof dish with a brush dipped in some softened butter.

2 Put the milk, cream and pesto in a large jug; whisk with a fork until combined. Season to taste with pepper.

3 If you have a V-slicer or mandoline, place the guard on one zucchini and slice thinly. Repeat with remaining zucchini. If you don't have a V-slicer, use a vegetable peeler to slice the zucchini as thinly as possible.

4 Peel potatoes with a vegetable peeler then slice them thinly using a mandoline, V-slicer or sharp knife. Make small piles of potato slices on a board; cut the piles in half lengthways so they are roughly the same height as the zucchini slices.

5 Arrange alternate slices of potato and zucchini in the dish so they are standing up on their sides. Pour the pesto mixture over the vegetables then sprinkle with the cheese. Place the dish on an oven tray; cover with greased foil.

6 Put the tray in the oven and bake about 30 minutes. Remove the foil, put the tray back in the oven and bake for 15 minutes more. Sprinkle the nuts over the vegetables and return to the oven; bake a further 15 minutes or until the top is golden and vegetables are tender.

prep + cook time 1½ hours
serves 6 as a side
nutritional count per serving
20.8g total fat
(11.4g saturated fat); 1229kJ
(294 cal); 17.4g carbohydrate;
8.2g protein; 2.8g fibre

tips Choose long, oval-shaped potatoes, to make slices as long as possible. You can peel the potatoes in advance and leave them in a bowl of cold water so they don't go brown. Once they are sliced, assemble the dish immediately. Don't stand the sliced potatoes in cold water or you will wash away their natural starch, which thickens the sauce.

serving ideas Goes well with barbecued lamb or grilled or steamed fish.

Cook the potatoes until they are soft when tested with a fork.

Pour the potatoes into a colander over the sink to drain off the water.

Mash potato with the butter and heated milk until smooth.

cheesy potato and spinach mash

1kg (2 pounds) potatoes

150g (4½ ounces) baby spinach leaves

1 cup (250ml) milk

60g (2 ounces) butter

1 cup (120g) coarsely grated cheddar cheese

1 Peel the potatoes with a vegetable peeler. Put the potatoes into a large saucepan; add enough cold water to the pan to completely cover the potatoes. Heat the pan on the stove over high heat until the water boils. Reduce the heat to medium-high and gently boil the potatoes, without a lid, for about 25 minutes or until the potatoes are soft when tested with a fork or skewer.

2 Pour the potatoes into a colander or sieve over the sink and drain off the water.

3 Meanwhile, coarsely chop the spinach.

4 Put the milk in a small microwave-safe jug; heat in the microwave on HIGH (100%) for about 30 seconds or until hot.

5 Return the drained potatoes to the saucepan. Turn the stove on to low and stir the potatoes for 1 minute to dry out. Remove from the heat.

6 Add the butter and hot milk to the potatoes, and mash with a potato masher until smooth. Stir the spinach and cheese into the mash. Season mash to taste with salt and pepper.

prep + cook time 40 minutes
serves 6 as a side
nutritional count per serving
16.8g total fat
(10.8g saturated fat); 1162kJ
(278 cal); 19.9g carbohydrate;
10.4g protein; 2.8g fibre

serving ideas Goes well with grilled steak, pork chops or barbecued sausages.

mashed peas

500g (1 pound) frozen peas

⅓ cup (80ml) pouring cream

30g (1 ounce) butter

1 Half-fill a large saucepan with water. Heat on the stove over high heat until the water boils. Add the peas to the pan and bring the water to the boil again. Carefully pour the peas into a colander or sieve over the sink and drain off the water.

2 Put the hot peas in a blender with the cream and butter; blend until smooth. Season to taste with salt and pepper.

prep + cook time 10 minutes
serves 4 as a side
nutritional count per serving
15.3g total fat
(9.9g saturated fat); 907kJ
(217 cal); 8.2g carbohydrate;
7.8g protein; 9.4g fibre

serving ideas · Goes well with meat pies or grilled steak.

Add peas to boiling water. Make sure the water is boiling as you add the peas, not off the boil.

Pour peas into a colander over sink to drain off the water.

Process the hot drained peas with the cream and butter until smooth.

Mix seasoning and coriander into the softened butter in a small bowl.

Place the butter mixture onto a piece of plastic wrap; roll to enclose the butter and shape it into a log.

Cut the cold butter in slices; serve with the corn.

mexican corn with spicy butter

125g (4 ounces) butter

2 teaspoons taco seasoning

1 tablespoon finely chopped fresh coriander (cilantro)

4 whole cobs of corn (1kg)

1 lime

1 Put the butter in a small bowl; stand at room temperature until softened.

2 Add the taco seasoning and coriander to the butter; mix with a teaspoon until combined. Spoon the butter onto a sheet of plastic wrap; roll to enclose and make a thick log. Refrigerate the butter until firm.

3 Remove the husk and silk from the corn; put the corn in a large microwave-safe bowl, cover the bowl with plastic wrap. Microwave on HIGH (100%) about 12 minutes or until the corn is tender.

4 Cut lime into wedges.

5 Carefully remove the corn from the microwave (the bowl will be hot). Get an adult to cut it into thirds for you, if necessary; serve with slices of the flavoured butter, some extra coriander leaves and lime wedges.

prep + cook time 25 minutes (+ refrigeration)
serves 6 as a side
nutritional count per serving
18.5g total fat
(11.4g saturated fat); 1160kJ
(277 cal); 20.1g carbohydrate;
5.2g protein; 5.5g fibre

tips You can buy ready-cut cobs of corn in the supermarket. Be careful when taking the corn out of the microwave as the bowl will be very hot; make sure you remove the plastic wrap cover away from you to allow the steam to escape. If you're in a hurry, you can place the soft log of butter in the freezer to firm up faster.

serving ideas Goes well with roasted chicken or grilled steaks.

potato and kumara bake

2 cloves garlic

¾ cup (180ml) milk

¾ cup (180ml) pouring cream

60g (2 ounces) cold butter

5 medium potatoes (1kg)

500g (1 pound) kumara
(orange sweet potato)

1 Preheat oven to 200°C/400°F. Brush the base and sides of a 2.25-litre (9-cup) square ovenproof dish with a brush dipped in some softened butter.

2 Peel and slice garlic. Heat the milk, cream and garlic in a small saucepan on the stove over a medium-high heat until the milk mixture is almost boiling. Remove from the heat.

3 Meanwhile, chop the butter into small cubes.

4 Peel the potatoes with a vegetable peeler and put them in a large bowl of cold water. Peel the kumara. If you have a V-slicer or mandoline, place the guard on one of the potatoes and slice thinly. Repeat with remaining potatoes and kumara. If you don't have a V-slicer, use a sharp knife or vegetable peeler to slice the vegetables as thinly as possible.

5 Arrange slices of potato, kumara and butter alternately in the dish; season with salt and pepper. Discard garlic from milk mixture; pour the milk mixture over the vegetables in the dish. Place the dish on an oven tray and cover with greased foil.

6 Put the tray in the oven and bake for 1 hour. Remove the foil from the dish and bake for a further 30 minutes or until the top is golden and potato is tender. Take the tray out of the oven and leave to cool for 10 minutes before serving.

prep + cook time 2 hours
serves 6 as a side
nutritional count per serving
22.6g total fat
(14.8g saturated fat); 1467kJ
(351 cal); 29.5g carbohydrate;
6.2g protein; 3.5g fibre

tips You can peel the potatoes in advance and leave them in a bowl of cold water so they don't go brown. Once they are sliced, assemble the dish immediately. Don't stand the sliced potatoes in cold water or you will wash away their natural starch, which thickens the sauce.

serving ideas Goes well with roasted lamb or beef, or grilled lamb chops.

Use a mandoline or V-slicer to slice the kumara and potato thinly.

Arrange potato and kumara in the dish so they overlap slightly with butter in between layers.

Pour the cream mixture over the vegetables in the dish.

Using a sharp knife, trim and discard the fat and rind from the bacon.

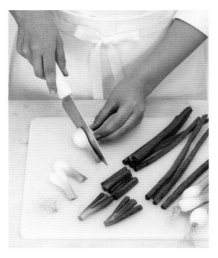

Trim the spring onions, then cut the green ends into 4cm lengths and cut the white bulbs cut in half.

Cook the bacon until browned. Add the onion and cook until soft, then add the peas to the pan.

braised peas with spring onion and bacon

5 cups (600g) frozen peas

6 shortcut bacon slices (150g)

6 spring onions (120g)

20g (¾ ounce) butter

½ cup (125ml) water

2 tablespoons finely chopped fresh flat-leaf parsley

1 Put the peas in a medium bowl and leave them until they have thawed.
2 Meanwhile, trim the rind and fat from the bacon and throw it away; chop the bacon coarsely.
3 Trim the onions. Cut the bottom third of the green ends into 4cm (1½-inch) lengths. Cut the white bulbs in half.
4 Heat the butter in a large saucepan on the stove over medium-high heat until melted. Add the bacon to the pan. Cook, stirring with a wooden spoon, for about 5 minutes or until the bacon is browned.
5 Add the onion to the pan; cook, stirring, for about 4 minutes or until the onion is softened. Add the peas and the water. Put a lid on the pan and cook for 5 minutes. Stir in the parsley. Season to taste with salt and pepper.

prep + cook time 20 minutes
serves 6 as a side
nutritional count per serving
5.4g total fat (2.7g saturated fat);
573kJ (137 cal);
7.2g carbohydrate;
11.4g protein; 8g fibre

serving ideas Goes well with grilled lamb or pork chops.

Test the cauliflower is tender with a fork or skewer. It should be easy to pierce when it's cooked.

Gradually add a little milk to the flour mixture; stir until smooth before adding the rest of the milk.

Once the sauce has boiled and thickened, take the pan off the heat and stir in the cheese.

cheesy cauliflower bake

1 small cauliflower (1kg)

2½ cups (625ml) milk

50g (1½ ounces) butter

¼ cup (35g) plain (all-purpose) flour

1½ cups (180g) coarsely grated cheddar cheese

pinch freshly grated nutmeg

2 tablespoons coarsely chopped fresh flat-leaf parsley

1 Preheat oven to 200°C/400°F.
2 Cut the leaves and large stem from the cauliflower and throw them away. Break the cauliflower into florets. Put the cauliflower into a large microwave-safe bowl, cover the bowl with plastic wrap. Microwave on HIGH (100%) for about 9 minutes or until the cauliflower is tender when tested with a fork or skewer.
3 Put the milk in a small microwave-safe jug; heat in the microwave on HIGH (100%) for about 30 seconds or until hot.

4 Meanwhile, heat the butter in a medium saucepan on the stove over medium heat until melted. Add the flour; stir with a wooden spoon until the mixture becomes a smooth paste. Pour the hot milk in slowly, a little at a time, and stir until the mixture is smooth before adding more milk. Stir the mixture over a medium to high heat until it boils and becomes thick.
5 Take the pan off the heat and add ½ cup of the cheese; stir the sauce until it is smooth. Add the nutmeg and season to taste with salt and pepper.
6 Put the cauliflower in a 1.25-litre (5-cup) dish; pour the cheese sauce over the cauliflower and sprinkle with the rest of the cheese. Place the dish on an oven tray.
7 Put the tray in the oven; bake about 30 minutes or until golden. Stand for 10 minutes before sprinkling with parsley to serve.

prep + cook time 50 minutes
serves 6 as a side
nutritional count per serving
21.5g total fat
(13.6g saturated fat); 1300kJ
(311 cal); 12.8g carbohydrate;
15.5g protein; 3.3g fibre

tips Be careful when taking the cauliflower out of the microwave as the bowl will be very hot; make sure you remove the plastic wrap cover away from you to allow the steam to escape. The sauce will thicken more quickly if the milk is heated before being stirred in gradually.

serving ideas Goes well with roast pork or grilled beef steaks.

mixed vegetable stir-fried rice

1½ cups (300g) white medium grain rice

2 cups (500ml) vegetable stock

250g (8 ounces) broccoli

1 large green capsicum (bell pepper) (350g)

4 celery sticks (600g)

4 green onions (scallions)

1 fresh corn cob (400g)

4 eggs

1 teaspoon dark soy sauce

2 teaspoons sesame oil

1 tablespoon vegetable oil

4cm (1½-inch) piece fresh ginger (20g), grated

1 Wash rice under cold running water until the water runs clear; drain well.
2 Combine rice and vegetable stock in medium saucepan, stir over high heat until mixture comes to the boil. Reduce heat to as low as possible, cover pan with a tight-fitting lid, cook 12 minutes.

Remove pan from heat; stand rice, still covered tightly, for 5 minutes. Remove lid, fluff rice with a fork.
3 Meanwhile, trim broccoli, cut into small florets. Cut top and bottom from capsicum, cut sides from capsicum, discard seeds and membranes; chop capsicum finely. Trim celery and green onions then slice finely, on the diagonal. Remove husk and silk from corn. Cut kernels from corn (get an adult to do this for you, if necessary).
4 Whisk eggs and sauce in a small bowl. Heat half the sesame oil in a large frying pan over medium heat; use absorbent paper to spread the oil over the base of the pan. Pour in half the egg mixture. Swirl pan to make a thin omelette. Slide omelette onto board; when cool, roll up tightly, then cut into thin strips. Repeat with remaining sesame oil and egg mixture.
5 Heat vegetable oil over high heat in same large pan; add all vegetables and ginger to pan.

6 Stir-fry vegetables until barely tender. Add rice to pan; stir-fry until rice is heated through. Season with salt and pepper; add omelette towards the end of the cooking time. Serve immediately.

prep + cook time 40 minutes
serves 6
nutritional count per serving
9.3g total fat
(1.8g saturated fat); 1508kJ
(360 cal); 52.6g carbohydrate;
13g protein; 6.2g fibre

tips This rice dish is delicious eaten on its own or served as a side with chicken or fish – this way, it would serve at least eight people. A squeeze of lemon or lime juice just before serving lifts the taste of the vegetables and rice. Don't squash the rice during the stir-frying, lift and turn the mixture over to keep it light and fluffy.

Prepare all the vegetables before starting to stir-fry. They should all be of a similar size.

Remove the omelette from the pan onto a board. Tightly roll the omelette then slice it thinly.

Lift the rice up and over with a fork to fluff it up before adding it to the pan with the vegetables.

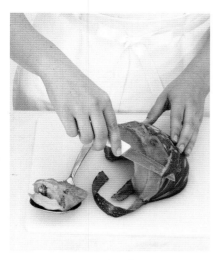

Microwave pumpkin for 3 minutes. When cool enough to handle, scoop out the seeds and cut away the skin.

Cut the pumpkin into wedges, and return it to the bowl. Microwave the pumpkin until it's soft.

Stir the polenta mixture until thick; stir in butter, cheese and pumpkin.

cheesy pumpkin polenta

750g (1½ pound) piece pumpkin

1 litre (4 cups) water

1 cup (170g) polenta

70g (2½ ounces) butter

1 cup (80g) coarsely grated parmesan cheese

1 Place the piece of pumpkin in a medium microwave-safe bowl, cover the bowl with plastic wrap. Microwave on HIGH (100%) for 3 minutes. Carefully remove the plastic wrap from the bowl. Remove the pumpkin from the bowl with tongs and put it on a board. When the pumpkin is cool enough to handle, cut away the skin; scoop out the seeds and throw them away. Cut the pumpkin into wedges.

2 Put the pumpkin back in the bowl, cover with plastic wrap. Microwave on HIGH (100%) for about 8 minutes or until the pumpkin is soft when tested with a fork or skewer. Drain the pumpkin in a colander in the sink then put it back in the bowl; mash with a potato masher until smooth.
3 Heat the water in a medium saucepan, covered with a lid, on the stove over high heat until the water boils. Gradually stir in the polenta with a wooden spoon. Reduce the heat to low so the polenta is simmering. Continue to stir for about 10 minutes or until the polenta is thick. Take the saucepan off the heat.
4 Add the butter, cheese and pumpkin to the polenta; stir until smooth. Season polenta to taste with salt and pepper. Sprinkle with extra cheese to serve

prep + cook time 20 minutes
serves 6 as a side
nutritional count per serving
14.9g total fat
(9.4g saturated fat); 1166kJ
(279 cal); 26g carbohydrate;
9.5g protein; 2g fibre

tip Be careful when taking the pumpkin out of the microwave as the bowl will be very hot; make sure you remove the plastic wrap cover away from you to allow the steam to escape.

serving ideas Goes well with roast pork or grilled pork chops.

desserts

pear tarts

30g (1 ounce) butter

1 sheet puff pastry

2 tablespoons caster (superfine) sugar

1 egg yolk

½ cup (60g) ground almonds

1 teaspoon vanilla extract

2 small pears (360g)

20g (¾ ounce) butter, extra

2 teaspoons caster (superfine) sugar, extra

1 tablespoon apricot jam (conserve)

2 teaspoons icing (confectioners') sugar

1 Have the butter at room temperature to soften.

2 Preheat oven to 220°C/425°F. Line a large oven tray with baking paper.

3 Put the pastry sheet on a board. Cut the pastry in half. Cut each half into three rectangles, about 8cm x 12cm (3¼-inches x 4¾-inches). Place the pastry rectangles on the oven tray, about 2.5cm (1-inch) apart.

4 Put the soft butter in a small bowl with the caster sugar and egg yolk. Stir with a wooden spoon or rubber spatula until the ingredients are mixed well. Stir in the ground almonds and extract.

5 Spread an equal amount of the almond mixture over each pastry rectangle, leaving a 1cm (½-inch) border around the edges.

6 Wash and dry the pears. Stand one pear upright on a board and slice thinly on two sides until you reach the core. Repeat with the remaining pear. Or, if you have a V-slicer or mandoline, place the guard on the pear and slice thinly on two sides and repeat with the remaining pear. Overlap pear slices on top of the almond mixture.

7 Melt the extra butter. Using a pastry brush, brush the pear lightly with the melted butter and sprinkle with the extra caster sugar.

8 Put the tarts in the oven and bake for 12 minutes or until the pastry is puffed and browned.

9 Warm the jam in a microwave safe bowl in microwave on HIGH (100%) for about 15 seconds. Brush pears with jam. Dust the tarts with sifted icing sugar before serving.

prep + cook time 35 minutes
makes 6
nutritional count per tart
19.7g total fat
(5.6g saturated fat); 1283kJ
(307 cal); 28.3g carbohydrate;
4.3g protein; 2.3g fibre

tip This recipe would also work really well with apple.

serving idea Serve with custard, ice-cream or cream.

Cut the pastry sheet in half. Cut each half into three rectangles.

Spread the almond mixture onto the pastry rectangles, leaving a 1cm border around the edges.

Slice the pears thinly on both sides until you reach the core.

Press the cornflake mixture over the base and side of the pie dish.

Sprinkle gelatine over water in a heatproof cup; place in a pan of simmering water

Whisk cream until soft peaks form; you can use a whisk, although using an electric beater is easier.

passionfruit and strawberry cheesecake

250g (8 ounces) cream cheese

6 cups (240g) corn flakes

⅓ cup (55g) icing (confectioners') sugar

100g (3 ounces) butter

1½ teaspoons powdered gelatine

1 tablespoon water

4 passionfruit

395g (12½ ounces) canned sweetened condensed milk

⅓ cup (80ml) lemon juice

⅔ cup (160ml) thickened (heavy) cream

250g (8 ounces) strawberries

1 Have the cream cheese at room temperature to soften.
2 Put the corn flakes in a large plastic resealable bag; crush the corn flakes with a rolling pin until fine. Empty the corn flakes into a medium bowl. Sift the icing sugar into the bowl.
3 Chop the butter; melt in a small saucepan on the stove over low heat. Add the butter to the corn flakes. Stir until mixed well.

4 Press the cornflake mixture over the base and 3cm (1¼ inch) up the side of a 24cm (9½-inch) pie dish. If the crumbs are difficult to press together, refrigerate the dish with the crumbs for 5 minutes and try again. Place the dish in the freezer to set the crust while making the filling.
5 Sprinkle the gelatine over the water in a small heatproof cup or jug; stand for 5 minutes, then place in a small saucepan with enough water to come about halfway up the side of the cup. Turn the stove on to low. Heat, stirring the gelatine until it dissolves. Take the cup out of the pan and place it on a board. Let the gelatine cool for 5 minutes.
6 Cut three of the passionfruit in half; scoop the pulp out with a teaspoon into a small bowl.
7 Beat the cream cheese in a small bowl with an electric mixer on medium speed until smooth. Add the condensed milk and lemon juice, beat until combined. Stop the mixer and scrape down the side and base of the bowl. Beat again until the ingredients are combined. Stir in the gelatine

mixture and passionfruit pulp. Transfer the mixture to a medium bowl. Clean the bowl.
8 Beat the cream in the cleaned bowl with an electric mixer until the cream has soft peaks. Stir the cream into the cream cheese mixture using a rubber spatula or wire balloon whisk. Spread the cream cheese mixture evenly over the corn flake crust. Refrigerate the cheesecake for about 6 hours or overnight until firm.
9 Trim hulls from the strawberries, cut the strawberries crossways into slices; top the cheesecake with the strawberry slices. Scoop the pulp from the remaining passionfruit and spoon it over the strawberries.

prep + cook time 40 minutes (+ refrigeration) **serves** 10
nutritional count per serving
24.2g total fat
(15.6g saturated fat); 1927kJ
(461 cal); 50.7g carbohydrate;
9.6g protein; 4.1g fibre

Break the eggs, one at a time, into a small cup or bowl, then pour into a medium bowl.

Carefully pour coconut mixture over apricots in dish.

To test if the pie is cooked, insert a knife into the centre, if it comes out clean, the pie is cooked.

apricot impossible pie

cooking-oil spray

1kg (2 pounds) canned apricot halves in natural juice

125g (4 ounces) butter

½ cup (75g) plain (all-purpose) flour

¾ cup (165g) caster (superfine) sugar

1 cup (80g) desiccated coconut

4 eggs

2 teaspoons vanilla extract

2 cups (500ml) milk

1 Preheat oven to 180°C/350°F. Spray a straight-sided 26cm (10½-inch) pie dish with cooking-oil spray.

2 Drain the apricots in a large strainer over a bowl. Stand for 5 minutes while making the coconut mixture.

3 Chop the butter; melt in a small saucepan on the stove over low heat (or in a microwave-safe bowl in the microwave on HIGH (100%) for about 30 seconds).

4 Sift the flour into a medium bowl. Stir in sugar and coconut.

5 Break the eggs, one at a time, into a small cup, then pour into a medium bowl. Add the extract and milk; whisk lightly until combined. Add the egg mixture and melted butter to the coconut mixture. Whisk until combined.

6 Put half the drained apricots in the base of the pie dish. Pour coconut mixture over apricots. Put the remaining apricots on top of the mixture. Put the dish on an oven tray; place in the oven for about 50 minutes or until the pie is browned lightly and set in the centre. To test if it is set, push a small sharp knife into the centre of the pie. Take the knife out; if the blade is clean, the pie is cooked. If it has uncooked egg mixture on it, return the pie to the oven for another 5 minutes. Serve the pie warm or cooled.

prep + cook time 1¼ hours
serves 10
nutritional count per serving 19.6g total fat (12.9g saturated fat); 1350kJ (323 cal); 30.2g carbohydrate; 6.4g protein; 2.7g fibre

note This easy-mix pie is called 'impossible' because it sorts itself out in the oven into three layers.

serving idea Serve with cream or ice-cream.

choc-mint mud cakes with ice-cream

These are quite small cakes, so you will need to serve each person two or three. Make sure you use a good quality ice-cream.

150g (5 ounces) dark eating (semi-sweet) chocolate

90g (3 ounces) butter

⅔ cup (160ml) water

1 cup (220g) firmly packed light brown sugar

2 eggs

⅔ cup (100g) self-raising flour

2 tablespoons cocoa powder

2 x 35g (1-ounce) peppermint crisp chocolate bars

1 litre (4 cups) vanilla ice-cream

1 Preheat oven to 170°C/340°F. Grease 12-hole (⅓-cup/80ml) standard muffin pan with a pastry brush dipped in soft butter. Brush the butter quite thickly over base and up the side of each hole.

2 Chop the chocolate and the butter coarsely. Heat the chocolate, butter and the water in a small saucepan on the stove over low heat, stirring until the mixture is smooth. Pour the chocolate mixture into a medium bowl. Stir in the sugar.

3 Break the eggs, one at a time into a small cup or bowl, then pour into a medium bowl. Whisk lightly until combined, then whisk eggs into chocolate mixture.

4 Sift the flour and cocoa over the chocolate mixture; whisk until combined. Divide the chocolate mixture equally into the pan holes.

5 Cut one chocolate bar in half lengthways. Cut each half into 6 pieces. Put one cut piece of chocolate (and some of the crumbled peppermint filling that may be left after you cut the bar) into the middle of each cake.

6 Put the pan in the oven; bake the cakes for about 30 minutes. To test if cakes are cooked, insert a skewer into the centre of the middle cake. If the skewer comes out clean, the cakes are cooked. Stand the cakes in the pan for 10 minutes to allow time for the cakes to become firm enough to be carefully removed from the pan. Use a metal spatula to loosen and remove the cakes.

7 Place warm cakes on serving plates. Top cakes with a scoop of ice-cream. Chop the remaining chocolate bar coarsely and sprinkle over the ice-cream and cakes.

prep + cook time 50 minutes (+ standing) **makes 12**
nutritional count per cake
16.5g total fat (11.7g saturated fat); 1388kJ (332 cal); 43.5g carbohydrate; 4.3g protein; 1g fibre

tips These cakes can be frozen for up to three months. To serve, thaw the cakes, then heat in the microwave on HIGH (100%) for about 20 seconds for each cake.

Brush the base and side of each pan hole of a 12-hole standard muffin pan with a pastry brush dipped in softened butter.

Cut one chocolate bar in half lengthways, then cut each length into 6 pieces (you should get 12 pieces from the chocolate bar).

Push one piece of chocolate, and some of the chocolate crumbs, into the centre of each cake.

Place thickly sliced bananas on the base of the oiled dish.

Mix flour, sugar, melted butter and milk together, then spread the mixture over the bananas.

Pour the sauce over the back of a spoon – this spreads the liquid over a larger area so it doesn't make holes in the top of the pudding.

banana butterscotch self-saucing pudding

cooking-oil spray

2 medium bananas (400g)

30g (1 ounce) butter

1 cup (150g) self-raising flour

½ cup (110g) firmly packed light brown sugar

½ cup (125ml) milk

butterscotch sauce

¾ cup (165g) firmly packed light brown sugar

1¾ cups (430ml) boiling water

60g (2 ounces) butter

1 Preheat oven to 180°C/350°F. Spray a 2-litre (8-cup) shallow ovenproof dish with oil spray.

2 Peel and thickly slice bananas. Place in the base of the dish.

3 Heat the butter in a small saucepan on the stove over low heat until melted.

4 Put the flour, sugar, melted butter and milk in a medium bowl; stir with a wooden spoon until combined. Spread mixture over the bananas.

5 Make the butterscotch sauce. Pour the sauce over the back of a spoon so that it spreads evenly over the mixture in the dish.

6 Put the dish on an oven tray; place in the oven. Bake the pudding for about 40 minutes or until the centre is firm. Stand the pudding on a board for 10 minutes before serving.

BUTTERSCOTCH SAUCE Stir all the ingredients with a wooden spoon in a medium heatproof jug until the sugar is dissolved.

prep + cook time 1¼ hours
serves 6
nutritional count per serving
12.6g total fat
(8.2g saturated fat); 1409kJ
(337 cal); 53.2g carbohydrate;
3.4g protein; 1.9g fibre

tip The pudding should be served straight after cooking as the sauce will be absorbed if left to stand.

serving idea Serve with thick cream or ice-cream.

Plating up ideas

Banana leaves Select leaves that are organic and free from blemishes and tears. Food can be either wrapped or served on the leaves. They are stocked by many Asian greengrocers.

Betel leaves The leaves of the betel plant, sold in bunches from Asian greengrocers, are great to hold or wrap bite-sized snacks.

Bowls in place of plates Brighten the table by using coloured bowls as serving dishes. Mix and match the colours for a bold, eye-catching, effect.

Witlof leaves are crisp and tightly furled with a fresh, slightly bitter, taste. They come as red- or green-tipped leaves and the cupped shape is great to serve finger food and small snacks.

Paper parcels This technique, also known as *en papillote*, steams food in a closed paper pouch made from baking paper or foil. The food is served in the pouch at the table.

Fabric Pieces of fabric make great table runners or mismatched place settings.

Small lettuce cups/leaves Crisp, cupped mild-tasting iceberg lettuce leaves can hold rice and mince dishes, and salads.

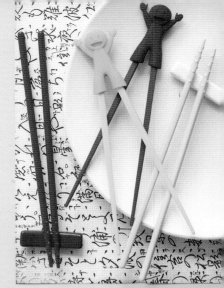

Sitting down for an authentic Chinese meal? These chopsticks are for those who need help.

Serving food in Chinese spoons These 'tasting' spoons hold just enough to leave you wanting more. Try prawns, dumplings, tiny sushi rolls, meatballs or fish cakes with a dipping sauce.

Drapery for plates Assorted mix and match fabrics are loud and flashy on the table.

Twirling pasta Using tongs, twirl the plate while gently lowering the pasta into a mound in the centre.

Cutlery Eating is fun, so add some fun to the cutlery as well. Bold colours in different designs lend a playful look to the setting.

Placemats Forget the tablecloth; the variety of designs available means you can have a different look each night.

Stack and drizzle Add height and depth to the food on the plate; differing heights are more visually appealing, but don't overcrowd the plate – start from the centre and leave room around the outside.

cooking techniques

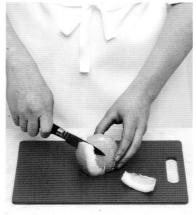

To shred a cabbage, cut it in half then peel and discard the outer leaves. Use a large flat knife to slice the cabbage into thin slices.

To toast sesame seeds in a wok or small frying pan, place seeds over medium heat, stir seeds, constantly, until fragrant and golden, about 3-5 minutes. Remove immediately from pan.

To peel an orange, cut the top and bottom off the orange. Stand the orange on its base and run a sharp knife down the orange, cutting off the peel and bitter white pith as you cut.

To segment an orange, cut off the skin and pith. Cut the orange in half lengthways, and cut out the segments between each membrane.

To blind bake, cover the pastry with baking paper; fill it with uncooked rice or dried beans. Cook the pastry for 10 minutes, then remove the paper and rice, and cook it a further 10 minutes, or until the pastry is golden.

To trim green onions, pull the papery skin, towards the root, off the onion. Cut the root end off, then slice the white end of the onion as directed by the recipe. The green end can be used to garnish the dish, either thinly sliced, or curled by placing thin strips into iced water.

To crush garlic, press unpeeled garlic firmly with the flat blade of a large knife (top) crushing the clove. Pull off the papery skin and chop the clove finely with the knife. A garlic press (bottom) removes and leaves the skin behind while crushing the garlic.

To remove corn kernels from fresh cobs, remove the husk (the outer covering) and the silk (the soft silky inner threads), and trim one side of the corn cob so it lies flat. Use a large flat-bladed knife to cut down the cob, close to the core, to remove the kernels.

To make a thin omelette for a stir-fry, pour the beaten egg into a lightly-oiled wok or frying pan; swirl the pan until the omelette is cooked.

To toast flaked almonds, stir nuts over a low heat in a dry frying pan until golden brown. Remove the nuts immediately from the pan to stop them from burning.

To slice a capsicum, cut the top and bottom off and stand it on one end; slice down removing all the flesh. Remove and discard the seeds and membranes, and slice the flesh.

To cut baby corn in half, use a sharp, pointed vegetable knife. Using a firm pressure, cut down through the centre of the corn towards the tip.

To peel an onion, cut the top end off the onion leaving the root end intact, then remove the papery outer skin. (You can also cut the onion in half before peeling.) Insert the knife under the skin, and lift and pull the skin towards the root following the curve of the onion.

To chop an onion, cut it in half through the root end (keep the root end intact as this holds the onion together, making it easier to slice). Lie the onion cut-side down and cut a number of slices into the onion (from front to back towards the root end) through the top of the onion. Next, cut the onion crossways (as if cutting into slices); the onion will fall into small cubes.

To separate an egg, set out two bowls. Crack the egg, and use your thumbs to gently pry the shell apart. Let the yolk settle in the lower half of the shell. Gently transfer the yolk back and forth between the shell halves, letting as much white as possible drip into the bowl. Be careful not to break the yolk. Place the yolk in a separate bowl.

To core and separate leaves from a lettuce, cut and discard the white core from the base of the lettuce. With the core-end facing down, smash the lettuce hard onto the board to loosen the outer leaves – they should come away easily in one piece.

glossary

ALMONDS flat, pointy-ended nuts with a pitted brown shell enclosing a creamy white kernel that is covered by a brown skin.
flaked paper-thin slices.
meal also known as ground almonds.

BACON RASHERS also known as bacon slices.
shortcut is a 'half rasher'; the streaky (belly), narrow portion of the rasher has been removed leaving the choice cut eye meat (fat end).

BAGEL CRISPS (bagel snacks) oven-baked thin bagel slices.

BASIL an aromatic herb; there are many types, but the most commonly used is sweet, or common, basil.
pesto a paste made from fresh basil, oil, garlic, pine nuts and parmesan.

BEANS
cannellini small white bean similar in appearance and flavour to other white beans (great northern, navy or haricot). Available dried or canned.
kidney medium-sized red bean, slightly floury in texture yet sweet in flavour; sold dried or canned, it's found in bean mixes and is the bean used in chilli con carne.
white in this book, some recipes may simply call for 'white beans', a generic term we use for canned or dried cannellini, haricot, navy or great northern beans, all of which can be substituted for each other.

BEEF
brisket a cheaper cut of beef from the belly; can be bought with or without bones as a joint for slow-roasting, or for stewing and casseroling.
chipolata sausages also known as 'little fingers'; highly spiced, coarse-textured beef sausage.
chuck comes from the neck and shoulder of the beef; tends to be chewy but flavourful and inexpensive. A good cut for braising or stewing.
gravy beef also known as shin beef.
shin (gravy beef) a boneless cut of beef from the lower shin; commonly used in stews and braises. Also known as a shank.

BREAD
ciabatta in Italian, the word means 'slipper', which is the traditional shape of this crisp-crusted white bread.

pitta also known as lebanese bread. This wheat-flour pocket bread is sold in large, flat pieces that separate into two thin rounds. Also available in small thick pieces called pocket pitta.
sourdough made by using a small amount of 'starter dough', which has the yeast culture and is mixed in with new flour and water. Part of this resulting dough is then saved to use as the starter next time.
tortillas thin, round, unleavened bread originating in Mexico. Two kinds are available, one made from wheat flour and the other from corn.

BREADCRUMBS
japanese also known as panko; gives a crunchy texture and a delicate, pale golden colour. Available in two kinds: larger pieces and fine crumbs. They have a lighter texture than Western-style breadcrumbs. Found in Asian grocery stores; nothing is an adequate substitution, although, if you can't find it substitute with stale breadcrumbs.
stale one- or two-day-old bread made into crumbs by blending or processing.

BUTTER use salted or unsalted butter; 125g is equal to one stick (4 ounces) of butter. *Unsalted butter*, often called 'sweet' butter, simply has no added salt. You can use regular butter in most cakes and baking, but it's advisable to stick to unsalted butter when it's called for in delicate toppings, icings etc.

BUTTER CHICKEN SIMMER SAUCE is tomato-based and quite rich, the addition of cream and butter giving it a thick, velvety texture.

BUTTERMILK originally the term given to the slightly sour liquid left after butter was churned from cream, today it is made similarly to yogurt. Sold alongside fresh milk products in supermarkets. Despite the implication of its name, it is low in fat.

BUTTERNUT PUMPKIN also known as squash; pear-shaped with golden skin and orange flesh.

CAPSICUM also known as bell pepper or, simply, pepper. Membranes and seeds must be discarded before use; comes in several colours, each of which has an individual flavour.
roasted available loose from delis, or packed in jars in oil or brine.

CARROTS, BABY also known as dutch carrots. Measuring about 5cm-8cm long, Sold in bunches with the leaves still attached.

CHICKEN
breast fillet breast halved, skinned and boned.
drumstick leg with skin and bone intact.
thigh skin and bone intact.
thigh cutlet skin and centre bone intact; sometimes found skinned with bone intact.
thigh fillet skin and centre bone removed.

CHIVES related to the onion and leek; has a subtle onion flavour. Chives and flowering chives are interchangeable.

CHOCOLATE, DARK EATING also known as semi-sweet or luxury chocolate; made of a high percentage of cocoa liquor and cocoa butter, and has a little added sugar.

COCONUT
cream is obtained commercially from the first pressing of the coconut flesh alone, without the addition of water; the second pressing (less rich) is sold as the milk. Available in cans and cartons at supermarkets.
desiccated concentrated, dried, unsweetened, finely shredded coconut.

CORELLA PEARS miniature dessert pear up to 10cm long.

CORIANDER a bright-green leafy herb also available ground or as seeds; these should not be substituted for fresh coriander as the tastes are completely different. The stems and roots of coriander are also used. Wash under cold water, removing any dirt; scrape the roots with a small flat knife to remove some of the outer fibrous skin. Chop roots and stems together to obtain the amount specified.

CORN CHIPS made from ground corn that's made into a dough, then rolled into a thin sheet, cut into shapes and toasted and fried until crisp.

CORN FLAKES manufactured cereal made of dehydrated then baked crisp flakes of corn. Also available as a finely ground mixture, 'crushed corn flakes', used for coating or crumbing food before frying or baking.

CREAM we use fresh cream, also known as pure and pouring cream, unless otherwise stated. It has no additives unlike commercially thickened cream. Minimum fat content 35%.
sour a thick commercially-cultured soured cream.
thickened a whipping cream containing a thickener. Minimum fat content 35%.

CUMIN also known as zeera or comino; resembling caraway in size, cumin has a spicy, nutty flavour. Available in seed form or dried and ground.

CURRY PASTE, MASSAMAN made from chilli and dried spices; has a much sweeter and milder flavour compared to other curries.

DILL also known as dill weed; used fresh, or dried in seed form or ground. Has a sweet anise/celery flavour. Its distinctive feathery, frond-like fresh leaves are grassier and more subtle than the dried version or the seeds.

EGGS we use 60g eggs in our recipes. When cracking eggs, crack one at a time into a cup, then pour into a larger bowl; we do this so if any egg is bad, it doesn't affect the whole lot.

FISH FILLETS, FIRM WHITE blue-eye, bream, flathead, swordfish, ling, whiting, jewfish, snapper or sea perch are all good choices. Check for any small pieces of bone in the fillets and use tweezers to remove them.

FIVE-SPICE POWDER a fragrant mixture of ground cinnamon, cloves, star anise, sichuan pepper and fennel seeds. Also known as chinese five-spice.

FLOUR
plain an all-purpose flour made from wheat.
self-raising plain flour sifted with baking powder in the proportion of 1 cup flour to 2 teaspoons baking powder. Also known as self-rising.

FRENCH-TRIMMED also sometimes just seen as 'frenched'; a butchers' term referring to a cutting method where all excess sinew, gristle and fat from the bone end of meat cutlets, racks or shanks are removed and the bones scraped clean.

GELATINE a thickening agent that is available in sheet form, known as leaf gelatine, or as a powder.

GINGER, GROUND also known as powdered ginger; used as a flavouring in cakes, pies and puddings but can't be substituted for fresh ginger.

GNOCCHI Italian 'dumplings' made with potatoes, semolina or flour; can be cooked in boiling water or baked with a sauce. Widely available dried, frozen, or fresh in vacuum sealed packages in supermarkets.

GREEK-STYLE YOGURT full-cream yogurt, often made from sheep milk; its thick, smooth consistency, almost like whipped cream, is attained by draining off the milk liquids.

LAMB BACKSTRAP the larger fillet from a row of loin chops or cutlets.

MAYONNAISE a rich, creamy dressing made with egg yolks, vegetable oil, mustard, and vinegar or lemon juice. We use whole egg mayonnaise in our recipes unless otherwise stated.

MINT a herb that includes many varieties including spearmint, common mint and peppermint. Spearmint has long, smooth leaves, and is the one that greengrocers sell, while common mint, with rounded, pebbly leaves, is the one that most people grow. Spearmint has the stronger flavour.

MIRIN a Japanese champagne-coloured cooking wine; made of glutinous rice and alcohol and used expressly for cooking. Should not be confused with sake.

MIXED SALAD LEAVES a mixture of assorted young lettuce and other green leaves; also known as mesclun.

NOODLES
crispy fried sold packaged (commonly a 100g packet), already deep-fried and ready to eat. Are sometimes labelled 'crunchy noodles', and are available in two widths: thin and spaghetti-like or wide and flat like fettuccine.
dried wheat these thin wheat noodles come as dried tangled cakes labelled 'mein' or 'instant noodles'. They are available from Asian grocery stores and most supermarkets.
hokkien also known as stir-fry noodles; fresh wheat noodles resembling thick, yellow-brown spaghetti needing no pre-cooking before being used.

NUTMEG the dried nut of an evergreen tree native to Indonesia; it is available in ground form or you can grate your own with a fine grater.

OIL
cooking spray we use a cholesterol-free spray made from canola oil.
olive made from ripened olives. Extra virgin and virgin are the best, while extra light or light refers to taste not fat levels.
peanut pressed from ground peanuts; the most commonly used oil in Asian cooking because of its high smoke point (it's capacity to handle high heat without burning).
sesame made from roasted, crushed, white sesame seeds.
vegetable sourced from plants.

PAPRIKA ground dried red capsicum (bell pepper); there are many types available, including sweet, hot, mild and smoked.

PARSLEY, FLAT-LEAF a flat-leaf variety of parsley also known as continental or italian parsley.

PASTA
lasagne sheets thinly rolled wide sheets of pasta; they do not require par-boiling prior to cooking.
macaroni small tube-shaped pasta.
rigatoni a form of tube-shaped pasta. Is larger than penne, usually ridged, and the tube's end does not terminate at an angle, like penne's does.
shell shell-shaped pasta ranging from tiny to very large in size.
spaghettini a very thin spaghetti, but thicker than vermicelli.
spiral a corkscrew-shaped pasta that's available in various sizes.

PASTRY
puff layers of dough and shortening (fat) are folded and rolled many times making many layers. When baked, it becomes a high, crisp, flaky pastry. *Butter puff pastry* uses butter for the shortening, whereas plain puff pastry uses a commercially made blend of vegetable and animal fats.
shortcrust a tender, crunchy, melt in the mouth buttery pastry. Once baked it is a light, crumbly easily broken pastry.

PEPPERMINT CRISP CHOCOLATE BAR a confectionery with a crisp centre of peppermint covered with a thin layer of chocolate.

PINE NUTS also known as pignoli; not, in fact, a nut but a small, cream-coloured kernel from pine cones.

POLENTA also known as cornmeal; a flour-like cereal made of dried corn (maize); sold ground in different textures; also the name of the dish made from it.

PORK
american-style pork ribs sold in long slabs or racks of 10 to 12 ribs, trimmed so that little fat remains. They are a long cut from the lower portion of the pig, specifically the belly and breastbone. These are often called american-style ribs and are the best ones to slather with barbecue sauce and cook on the barbie.
fillets skinless, boneless eye-fillet cut from the loin.
italian sausage a coarse pork sausage, generally sold in plump links. Usually flavoured with garlic and fennel or anise seed. It comes in two styles – hot (flavoured with thai red chilli) and sweet (without the added heat). It must be well cooked before serving.
prosciutto cured, air-dried (unsmoked), pressed ham.

PRAWNS also known as shrimp. Varieties include, school, king, royal red, sydney harbour and tiger. Can be bought uncooked (green) or cooked, with or without shells.

RICE
arborio small, round-grained rice, absorbs a large amount of liquid.
basmati a fragrant long-grained white rice. Wash several times before use.
jasmine fragrant long-grained white rice; white rice can be substituted, but will not taste the same. Has a subtle floral aroma.

SALMON FILLET has a red-pink firm flesh with few bones and a moist delicate flavour.
smoked found sliced in supermarkets.

SAUCE
barbecue a spicy, tomato-based sauce used to marinate or baste.
fish also called nam pla or nuoc nam; made from pulverised salted fermented fish, most often anchovies. Has a pungent smell and strong taste.
oyster Asian in origin, this rich, brown sauce is made from oysters and their brine, cooked with salt and soy sauce, and thickened with starches.

soy made from fermented soya beans. Several variations are available in most supermarkets and Asian food stores. *Japanese soy* is an all-purpose low-sodium soy sauce made with more wheat than its Chinese counterparts; fermented in barrels and aged. Possibly the best table soy, and the one to choose if you only want one variety. *Light soy* is a fairly thin, pale, but salty tasting, sauce; used in dishes in which the natural colour of the ingredients is to be maintained. Don't confuse with salt-reduced or low-sodium soy sauces.
sweet chilli a comparatively mild, Thai-style sauce made from red chillies, sugar, garlic and vinegar.
Tabasco brand name of an extremely fiery sauce made from vinegar, thai red chillies and salt.
teriyaki a Japanese sauce made from soy sauce, mirin, sugar, ginger and other spices.
tomato also known as ketchup or catsup; made from tomatoes, vinegar and spices.
tomato pasta made from a blend of tomatoes, herbs and spices.
worcestershire a dark coloured condiment made from garlic, soy sauce, tamarind, onions, molasses, lime, anchovies, vinegar and seasoning.

SAUSAGES minced (ground) meat seasoned with salt and spices, mixed with cereal and packed into casings. Also known as snags or bangers.

SESAME SEEDS black and white are the most common of this small oval seed, however there are red and brown varieties also.

STOCK available in cans, bottles or tetra packs. Stock cubes or powder can be used. As a guide, 1 teaspoon of stock powder or 1 small crumbled stock cube mixed with 1 cup water will give a fairly strong stock. Be aware of the salt and fat content of stock cubes, powders and prepared stocks.

SUGAR
brown an extremely soft, finely granulated sugar retaining molasses for its characteristic colour and flavour.
caster also known as superfine or finely granulated table sugar.
icing also known as confectioners' sugar or powdered sugar; granulated sugar crushed together with a small amount of added cornflour.

white a coarse, granulated table sugar, also known as crystal sugar.

SWEETENED CONDENSED MILK from which 60% of the water has been removed; the remaining milk is then sweetened with sugar.

TACO SEASONING MIX found in most supermarkets; is meant to duplicate the taste of a Mexican sauce made from oregano, cumin, chillies and other spices.

TAHINI sesame seed paste; most often used in hummus, baba ghanoush and other Middle-Eastern recipes.

TOMATO PASTE triple-concentrated tomato puree.

TURMERIC, GROUND has a deep orange-yellow colour and is commonly used as a spice in curries and to impart color to mustard and other dishes. It has a distinctly earthy, slightly bitter, slightly hot peppery flavour and a mustardy smell.

VANILLA EXTRACT made by extracting the flavour from the vanilla bean pod; the pods are soaked, usually in alcohol, to capture their flavour.

VERJUICE unfermented grape juice with a fresh lemony-vinegar flavour. It's available in supermarkets, usually in the vinegar section.

VINEGAR
cider (apple cider) made from crushed fermented apples.
rice a colourless vinegar made from fermented rice and flavoured with sugar and salt. Also known as seasoned rice vinegar.
rice wine made from rice wine lees (sediment left after fermentation), salt and alcohol.

WATERCRESS one of the cress family, also known as winter rocket. A large group of peppery greens used raw in salads, dips and sandwiches, or cooked in soups. Highly perishable, so use as soon as possible after purchase.

WHOLEGRAIN MUSTARD also known as seeded mustard. A french-style coarse-grain mustard made from crushed mustard seeds and dijon-style french mustard.

ZUCCHINI also known as courgette; small, pale- or dark-green, yellow or white vegetable belonging to the squash family.

index

First published in 2012

ACP Books are published by ACP Magazines Limited,

a division of Nine Entertainment Co.

54 Park St, Sydney

GPO Box 4088, Sydney, NSW 2001.

phone (02) 9282 8618; fax (02) 9267 9438

acpbooks@acpmagazines.com.au; www.acpbooks.com.au

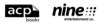

ACP BOOKS

Publishing Director, ACP Magazines · Gerry Reynolds

Publisher · Sally Wright

Editor-in-Chief · Susan Tomnay

Creative Director · Hieu Chi Nguyen

Food Director · Pamela Clark

Published and Distributed in the United Kingdom by Octopus Publishing Group

Endeavour House

189 Shaftesbury Avenue

London WC2H 8JY

United Kingdom

phone (+44)(0)207 632 5400; fax (+44)(0)207 632 5405

info@octopus-publishing.co.uk;

www.octopusbooks.co.uk

Printed by Toppan Printing Co., China

International foreign language rights, Brian Cearnes, ACP Books bcearnes@acpmagazines.com.au

A catalogue record for this book is available from the British Library.

ISBN 978-1-907428-68-5

© ACP Magazines Ltd 2012

ABN 18 053 273 546